> # You must be the change you wish to see in the world.
> ## —Mahatma Gandhi

Through the stories and advice of hundreds of business and government leaders, celebrities, and average citizens, BE THE CHANGE! explores each person's capacity to change the world. Intertwining practical tips on service and volunteerism with real-life stories of personal transformation, BE THE CHANGE! reveals how involvement in service can not only change the world, but also change an individual's life.

Editor Michelle Nunn, CEO and cofounder of Hands On Network, offers reflections to create a narrative of hope. The book provides practical advice, inspiration, and humor. Through these stories, readers can begin to take their own journey of service and discovery.

Hands On Network is a growing movement of engaged citizens who are making a tangible difference in the country and the world. Hands On N hundreds of thousands of volunteers throug national and international affiliates. The Ne manages nearly 50,000 projects a year, from chair ramps in San Francisco and teaching reading in Atlanta to rebuilding homes and lives in the Gulf Coast communities.

*A portion of the proceeds from the sale of this book will go to support Hands On Network's activities.*

BE THE CHANGE!

# BE THE CHANGE!

Change the World. Change Yourself.

EDITED BY MICHELLE NUNN

**Hundreds of Heads Books, LLC**
Atlanta

Library of Congress Cataloging-in-Publication Data

Be the change! : change the world, change yourself / Michelle Nunn, editor.
     p. cm.
  Includes bibliographical references and index.
  ISBN 1-933512-00-8 (alk. paper)
  1.  Helping behavior. 2.  Altruism. 3.  Change (Psychology)  I. Nunn,
Michelle.
  BF637.H4B4 2006
  158'.3--dc22
                                        2006027433

HUNDREDS OF HEADS* books are available at special discounts when purchased in bulk for premiums or institutional or educational use. Excerpts and custom editions can be created for specific uses. For more information, please e-mail sales@hundredsofheads.com or write to:

HUNDREDS OF HEADS BOOKS, LLC
#230
2221 Peachtree Road, Suite D
Atlanta, Georgia 30309

ISBN-10: 1-933512-00-8
ISBN-13: 978-193351200-6

Printed in U.S.A.
10 9 8 7 6 5 4 3 2 1

# CONTENTS

# FOREWORD

PEOPLE OFTEN ASK ME WHO IS THE MOST MEMORABLE PERSON I've ever interviewed. I think they expect me to answer Mikhail Gorbachev, Ronald Reagan, Dr. Martin Luther King Jr., Bobby Kennedy, Margaret Thatcher, Nelson Mandela, Golda Meir, or another of the big-name leaders I've interviewed in my 40 years in journalism.

But the most memorable people were the ordinary folks who showed great courage in difficult circumstances and expected no recognition: brave young black and white civil rights workers in the South during the 1960s; those who answered their country's call and went to war in Vietnam and those who answered their conscience and did not go, willingly accepting the legal consequences; a young white physician in an all-black squatters' camp in South Africa, working night and day in a primitive medical shelter at the height of apartheid; the many young Americans I encounter around the world, working for Save the Children or the International Rescue Committee in desperate circumstances.

They are all honoring the legacy of what I call the Greatest Generation, the young men and women who came of age during the Great Depression, when life was about sacrifice and sharing. Just as they were beginning to emerge from that difficult time, they were summoned, at home and abroad, to fight the greatest war in the history of mankind. They did that with great sacrifice, common cause, and few complaints.

When the war was over and the world had been saved, they came home to marry in record numbers, go to college in record numbers, build new industries, and give us new medicine, new art, and new hope. Moreover, they did something unprecedented in the long history of warfare: They rebuilt their enemies and gave the vanquished a fresh opportunity to reclaim their equality and their place in a world of law.

It would have been easy for the Greatest Generation to lay down their arms and say, "I've done my share. I'm going home to worry only about me." But they did not. They returned to serve their communities, their churches, their temples, their states, and their nation, expanding the rights of those who had been left behind too long and dedicating their lives to what Thomas Jefferson called the common welfare.

Now a new generation is taking their place, a generation of young people empowered with the tools of a transformational technology: personal computers, the Internet, cell phones, and satellites. But the best of them know there is no delete button for poverty, no insert button for morality, no cut and paste for tolerance. They know from the lessons left behind by their parents and grandparents that life is most rewarding when the boots are on the ground and hands are extended to care for others.

Tom Brokaw

# INTRODUCTION

MAHATMA GANDHI, MARTIN LUTHER KING JR., Mother Teresa, Jonas Salk, Clara Barton: These are hallowed names of people who live in our historical imagination. Yet none of them held elected office. None of them ran corporations or made millions of dollars. Although our society admires celebrity and material reward, those whom we most revere give of themselves and make a difference for others. The problem is that these iconic figures have become so lionized that it is impossible to aspire to be like them. They seem to be of another world, one of superheroes and saints. Yet the transformations they achieved—in the world and in themselves—*are* within our reach.

I have seen firsthand that ordinary people are capable of superhero-like accomplishments. My hope is that this book prompts you to believe that you can, in the words of Gandhi, "be the change you wish to see in the world."

We live in a world of self-help, but the most profound and fundamental way to help ourselves lies in our ability to reach out and help others—to extend beyond our own needs to support those around us. *Be the Change!* shows just how diverse and unlimited the opportunities to serve really are. It portrays, with a light and, we hope, inspiring sensibility, the gratification, fun, and humor to be found on the journey of service.

There are many ways to use and enjoy this book—you may want to read it cover to cover, stopping along the way to volunteer. You can pick it up, let it fall open where it will, and let a story lead you to ponder the deep human connections that service experiences provide. You can use it as a point of reference to plan your next service project. You'll find books to read and Web sites to visit. However you approach this book, we hope it will cause you to reflect or inspire you on a service journey of your own. Perhaps you'll jot down some notes in the margin and share your copy of the book with others.

Our world is different as a result of countless service leaders. There is a profound truth in Martin Luther King Jr.'s familiar pronouncement that "everybody can be great because everybody can serve." Service is the great equalizer.

In this book you will hear from persons, some celebrated and some not, who are embracing their capacity to make a difference. They all remind us that we each have remarkable gifts and that we discover our greatest selves when we reach out beyond ourselves.

Millions of acts of courage and imagination have gone into shaping a world in which democracy and self-governance is increasingly the norm, where science and medicine have the power to cure ills and ensure longevity, where technology unites us in a global web of communication and learning that promises an even faster pace of change and possibility for progress. We stand at a time of enormous potential, but also of danger—environmental hazards, nuclear proliferation, global poverty, and terrorism are all very real threats to our world and the promise of progress. But perhaps the biggest obstacle of all is apathy.

We need to participate—within our communities and in our democracy. Individual acts of daring and creativity will ultimately determine the fate of nations and our increasingly global society. And those acts will change us in return. We often think that certain issues or problems are beyond our capacity to solve. But in the words of the Hopi Indian elders, "We are the ones we've been waiting for." May the words and acts of the ordinary superheroes and saints in the pages of this book help us all discover that we too have the power to change the world, and to change ourselves in the process.

Michelle Nunn

# CHAPTER 1

# Sparks that ignite the spirit
## MOTIVATION TO SERVE

WHAT LEADS US TO ACT IN SERVICE TO OTHERS? What compels us to want to change our world, and to believe that we can? Sometimes single moments can change our lives—a glimpse into someone else's world that enables us to truly empathize and to want to help.

Often the initial spark can be the realization of our own power to make a difference. We must believe that we can make a difference in order to feel compelled to act. Or that spark might be awakening to our own vulnerability, through tragedy or death.

While a single moment can be a catalyst, a lifetime of preparation helps create the framework for our service lives. Whether they realize it or not, most people's decisions to serve are influenced by people and events in their past. I have seen many people inspired to serve as a tribute to the legacy of ancestors and mentors who have gone before them. They want to repay service they have received or to emulate role models they have loved.

# BE THE CHANGE!

Many are prompted to act for the sake of their children and the generations ahead of them. Others want to thank the world for the blessings of their lives. And while many act from a place of privilege, it is perhaps most inspiring to hear from people who find a way to serve others when they themselves are suffering. The opportunity to serve others is available to all—across income levels and geography and circumstance.

Often the first steps of our service journey are the beginning of our own personal transformation, opening us up to experiences beyond anything we ever imagined. However we get started, in helping others, we move beyond ourselves and find ourselves renewed.

**On 9/11, I sat in front of my television,** transfixed as I grappled with the horrific images that were unfolding before my eyes. Some eight hours later, I received a call telling me my good friend, Lisa Frost, had been on United Airlines Flight 175, the second hijacked plane to strike the World Trade Center. As if the cloak had been flung off, I began to see for the first time the injustices in the world, in our societies, and in my backyard. I was determined to find answers, to fight for a better world. In doing so, I spent the next two years as an AmeriCorps Promise Fellow, asking more questions, tackling the world hands-on.

Roger Wong
Boston, Massachusetts

**My parents are Holocaust survivors.** After the war, when my father was about 21, he traveled across Europe and then the United States. From Budapest to Austria to California, my father and his siblings were amazed at the generosity and efficiency of the volunteer organizations that aided them. People were just waiting to feed, clothe, and house Jewish refugees. My father still speaks fondly of the members of the Jewish community in California (where I still live and work) who "adopted" his family when they arrived in this country. His experience with volunteers is part of my inspiration to serve.

> "The greatest good you can do for another is not just share your riches, but reveal them their own."
> Benjamin Disraeli

Lisa Tabak
San Francisco, California

3

**When I was in seventh grade,** I was nice to a boy everyone picked on. I stuck up for him when people teased him, and I talked with him on the way to class. When I moved away that summer, he gave me a picture, a letter, and a small crystal pendant. In his letter he told me how much of a difference I had made for him. I learned that his parents had passed away three years before, and he was living with his 20-year-old sister. They didn't have money for new clothes, and he was constantly teased. He gave me the crystal to remind me to let my light shine, because someone will see it and it will brighten their day.

Corinne Carlson
Granite Falls, Washington

"You cannot do a kindness too soon, for you never know how soon it will be too late."
Ralph Waldo Emerson

**When I was in grade school,** there was a woman near my home in Indiana named Mrs. Jenny. She was our crossing guard, and she crossed me every day on the way to school and on the way home. She was always so nice! Every afternoon she would stop and ask me what I learned that day and how my day went. I used to go home and tell my mother that one day I wanted that job. Now I have it: For the past 10 years, I've been a volunteer crossing guard for the local school district.

Judith Brendel
Watts Flats, New York

**In 1996, a coworker of mine** was diagnosed with AIDS. He asked for my help because he was alone. I hesitated; I had a two-year-old daughter, had a homophobic husband, and did not know much about AIDS. What little I did know made me nervous.

I decided to do it. I never guessed it would change the course of my life. When we were out shopping, walking, eating in restaurants, people would point at us, turn up their noses, and move out of our way, as if the sores, blisters, and pain were something Dennis had consciously chosen for himself. They were scared and ignorant about the devastation he was suffering. Each time this happened, I'd rub Dennis on the back and tell him not to worry, because God had his back, and I did too.

Until his death, I continued to visit with Dennis, read to him from his Bible, comfort him, and cook him nutritious meals. I promised him I would make a difference in the world and help in the fight against AIDS. In the fall of 1997, I launched a community newsletter, *KONSHES JUNGK* (conscious junk), to educate the urban community with facts about AIDS, stories about Dennis, and other important information.

Kristen Yolas
Sherman Oaks, California

**When my nephew was nine years old,** he was diagnosed with type 1 diabetes. As I watched my sister scramble to find as much information as she could to try to help him adjust to this sudden and massive life change, I knew I needed to help. Every year since, I have contributed financially, and I also try to raise awareness for the need for diabetes research.

Karri Moss
Pinckneyville, Illinois

Diabetes is a disease in which the body does not produce or properly use insulin. In the United States, 20.8 million people, or 7 percent of the population, have diabetes. Nearly one-third of these people are unaware that they have the disease. For more information, visit the Web site of the American Diabetes Association, www.diabetes.org.

## Voices of Change:
## Congressman John Lewis

IN DECEMBER OF 1955, I heard about Rosa Parks and the bus boycott. I followed what was happening, the drama of it. I listened to Dr. King on the radio, and I felt like he was speaking to me. I felt like he was saying, "John Lewis, you can make a contribution." I felt like it was a calling. It was a mission. I had an obligation.

I never thought, along the way, of turning back or deviating from my mission or calling. When I was growing up, it was my goal to become a minister. I went to school and studied religion and philosophy. I thought it was a calling, but Dr. King and Rosa Parks came along, and I moved in a different direction. Even today I see my involvement in the rights movement and in electoral politics as an extension of my early calling to the ministry. It's an extension of my faith. I believe you've been planted on this little bit of earth to do something and try to make a difference. JFK said, "We all can make a difference and every person should try."

In my own little way, I tried to do something. I asked my mother and father during the 1940s and 1950s about segregation and discrimination. They said, "That's the way it is. Don't get in the way." Now I tell people, "I got in the way. I got in trouble. You need to get in the way."

And because of this, I've met people along the way who have inspired me: Dr. King and Rosa Parks and Robert Kennedy. I've also had an opportunity to meet Mother Teresa when she came to the Capitol, and I met Nelson Mandela. My life has allowed me to see countless individuals that did what I call "get in the way." I tell young people today to get in the way. You have to give something back. You have to try to do some good. Forget about your own circumstances and get involved in the circumstances of others.

Continue to go for it. Continue to follow your heart and passion. Follow your compass. Do what you can with others to create a community that is not just local or national but is a world community at peace with itself.

*In 1977, Congressman John Lewis was appointed by President Jimmy Carter to direct more than 250,000 volunteers of ACTION, the federal volunteer agency. He has since been the recipient of numerous awards, including the Preservation Hero Award given by the National Trust for Historic Preservation, the Martin Luther King Jr. Non-Violent Peace Prize, the President's Medal of Georgetown University, the John F. Kennedy Profile in Courage Award for lifetime achievement, and the National Education Association Martin Luther King Jr. Memorial Award. The Timberland Company has established the John Lewis Award, which honors humanitarian service, and has established a John Lewis Scholarship Fund.*

# BE THE CHANGE!

**On the Friday before Labor Day,** 1991, my husband, our four-year-old son, Christopher, and I were going to Myrtle Beach for the long weekend. Several days before, I'd had my annual physical and was expecting the usual call from my doctor pronouncing me completely healthy. Instead, I found out I had cervical cancer and would, in all likelihood, undergo a hysterectomy. I was only 24 years old.

That diagnosis changed my life forever. I began volunteering with the American Cancer Society. I first called them to get information about my type of cancer, but I quickly realized I might be able to help others after they were diagnosed with cancer. I volunteered with them for nearly five years. My life has been rewarded a hundred times over for my involvement as a volunteer.

Deborah Ray
Cayce, South Carolina

**The American Cancer Society is a nationwide, community-based voluntary health organization. Headquartered in Atlanta, Georgia, it has state divisions and more than 3,400 local offices. For more information, visit www.cancer.org.**

**I heard a story on the news about a dog** that had been hit by a car and transported to a vet hospital, but no surgery would be performed until the dog's $3,000 vet bill was paid. The dog would be put to sleep if no action was taken, so I paid the bill and walked out of the clinic a new person.

I now volunteer my time collecting ladies' shoes and bags for my organization, Purses for Pups and Heels for Hounds. I sell the items on eBay and give 100 percent of the proceeds for medical care, rehabilitative treatment, and food for hurt and abandoned animals across the country.

Cynthia McKay
Castle Rock, Colorado

# Editor's Note on Service and Faith

Across all of the great faith traditions, we find absolute align-
ment and clarity around the example of service and the com-
mandment to serve others. Moses, Jesus, Krishna, Buddha,
and Muhammad all lived out the life of service. They manifest
the divine, not through their temporal power or wealth, but
through the powerful example of their sacrifice and service to
others. Jesus healed the sick and ministered to the poor and
the needy. Buddha sought to alleviate the suffering of the
world through his own personal transformation and by sharing
these principles with the world. Muhammad gave away his
wealth in order to live in solidarity with the poor. Throughout
this section and the entire book you will find that people are
inspired to act out of the faith and value of their religious
traditions. This is a powerful platform for people of all faiths
to unite in action.

**In 1975, my parents fled Vietnam.** A church in Lynchburg, Virginia, took them in and sponsored my family. While I don't know all the details, I know the community took us under their wing, helping us financially and helping my parents learn about the United States. They taught my mom how to drive and helped us learn English. I think of my involvement in volunteering as the ultimate thank-you to those people who helped my family.

Brenda Tran
Atlanta, Georgia

**My father was a volunteer** fireman for 35 years and really fostered my interest in firefighting. He used to tell my brother and me all kinds of stories about fires that he had to fight. I'm sure there was a lot of embel-lishment going on, but he really knew how to capture our attention.

I couldn't wait until I was 16 so I could become a junior firefighter. A couple of years after that, I became a full-fledged firefighter. Seeing how important it was to my father and hearing him describe how important the job was led me to follow in his footsteps.

Nathan Bernarding
Jamestown, New York

**When my son was born,** I "got it": I had to leave the world a better place for him and his friends. I could no longer walk this earth without actively engaging in the process of change. While I have done service in the past, my motivation has changed. I do it even if it's inconvenient or if I'm tired. It's the price for having brought another life into this world; an obligation.

Nikki Monacelli
Chattaroy, Washington

**I play the flute and my sister** plays the violin. When we were both younger, we would go with our grandmother to visit an elderly friend of hers. While we were there, we would always be asked to play at least one song for the woman. I was not thrilled to do this, being shy, but we continued for about a year.

When the woman passed away, my sister and I didn't really think much about it and went on with our lives as usual. Later that week, my parents got a phone call from the woman's lawyer, saying that she had left her piano to my sister and me. Each time I play it or even glance in its direction, I'm reminded to take a little time to do something nice for another person.

Krista Baptist
Colorado Springs, Colorado

**My father is a Holocaust survivor** and lost many relatives in the Holocaust, so I'm very passionate about Holocaust education. I realized there are very few people left who can transmit their stories from this terrible era, so I decided to volunteer for a group of Holocaust survivors that meets once a month in the city. I feel it's important for me to act as a witness to their experience, and I also feel lucky to have this opportunity.

Andrea Syrtash
New York, New York

"Those who are not looking for happiness are the most likely to find it, because those who are searching forget that the surest way to be happy is to seek happiness for others.
Martin Luther King Jr.

11

## Voices of Change:
## Kareem Abdul-Jabbar

"

While I was in grade school, I observed the civil rights battles that were taking place on a daily basis across America. Some of the more violent events were very disturbing to me, and they made me wonder if there ever could be real peace and justice in America. At times, I thought that America's history on racial matters could not be overcome.

Fortunately, I was given a very simple but profound lesson on the subject by my high school basketball coach, Jack Donahue. The rights and wrongs of race relations were not the first things that came to mind when you considered a basketball coach. But Coach Donahue said something that hit home and that has stayed with me my whole life. He said that color and social status were accidents of birth and things we could not control. But what we did with our lives from the time that we do have control meant everything. The quality of people was the only basis you could use to judge their worth as human beings. Everything else is superficial.

This outlook has helped me understand people and situations throughout my life. Coach Donahue has passed on, but his wisdom helps me every day. When I decided to write my book *Black Profiles in Courage,* I hoped to find my niche and affect society in a positive way. One of the most satisfying experiences I've had came when a gentleman in Oklahoma City approached me to thank me for writing *Black Profiles in Courage.* He had used my book as a source for bedtime stories for his two daughters, and he was convinced that their confidence and pride as black Americans came from the knowledge that he took from my book.

*Kareem Abdul-Jabbar's patented skyhook helped him and the Los Angeles Lakers earn a staggering five NBA championships (1980, 1982, 1985, 1987, and 1988). He earned another three NBA MVP awards in 1976, 1977, and 1980, a record six in total, and was named* Sports Illustrated's *Sportsman of the Year in 1985. Upon his retirement in 1989, Abdul-Jabbar was a leader in nine NBA statistical categories, including points scored (38,387), seasons played (20), playoff scoring (5,762), MVP awards (6), minutes played (57,446), games played (1,560), field goals made and attempted (15,837 of 28,307), and blocked shots (3,189).*

**All community service work** is a mechanism for something else. I travel with a band of students who play at international fund-raisers for the Make-A-Wish Foundation. It's a really high-level jazz band, and they have all these honors. So what? It's not about the music and, really, it's not even just about the sick kids. The most important thing about this project is that we're teaching these students about humanity, about other cultures. We are showing them that the world does not revolve around Fort Lauderdale, that there is a huge world out there. And *that's* a big deal.

Danny Lieberman
Fort Lauderdale, Florida

A network of more than 25,000 volunteers enable the Make-A-Wish Foundation to serve children with life-threatening medical conditions. Volunteers serve as wish granters, fund-raisers, special events assistants, and in numerous other capacities. Visit www.wish.org for more information.

**When I was in sixth grade,** my teacher stayed after school every day with a group of us to teach us algebra. We lived in a poor neighborhood, with few healthy options for entertaining ourselves. His influence and confidence made such a difference in my development. I want to return that kindness to another generation.

Trinette Marquis
Sacramento, California

**I came here from Kenya in 1995** to attend college. I remember reading in the local newspaper about an 11-year-old who had shot someone. I couldn't believe that an 11-year-old had a gun, let alone had shot someone! I thought that I should do something to help. So I began volunteering at the Boys & Girls Clubs, helping kids with their homework.

Erastus Mong'are
Newark, Delaware

**When I was a practicing psychotherapist,** I worked with a number of female clients dealing with issues of self-esteem, which manifested as an inability to speak up for themselves both in the workplace and relationships. One afternoon, a colleague and I fantasized about a self-esteem curriculum for young girls that could be used in camps and schools. It would work toward preventing this loss of voice that we were seeing in our female clients. That conversation was the seed for GOAL—even though it took almost a year from that conversation before the seed began to germinate.

We worked for a year on our curriculum before we ever ran any programs. The first program, in the summer of 1998, was a residential camp with 25 girls from very diverse backgrounds. Subsequently, we added more programs, including backpacking wilderness adventures and mother/daughter weekends, serving approximately 150 girls each year. We now partner with other organizations and institutions that serve girls to implement our curriculum.

My hope for GOAL is that it will continue to grow and that the girls we are serving today will become the leaders of tomorrow, secure in who they are, respectful of the differences they find in others, and able to move the world forward by bridging those differences.

Kaffie McCullough
Atlanta, Georgia

In every community, boys and girls are left to find their own recreation and companionship in the streets. Young people need to know that someone cares about them. Boys & Girls Clubs of America programs and services promote and enhance the development of boys and girls by instilling in them a sense of competence, usefulness, belonging, and influence. Visit www.bgca.org for more information.

# BE THE CHANGE!

**I was led to serve others** when I was laid off from my job as a flight attendant. It was a job I deeply loved and I was distraught over having lost it. I thought that volunteering would help me overcome my feelings of self-pity. Focusing my energy on serving others not only gave me a purpose in life at a time when I felt I had none, it helped me to see that my situation wasn't as bad as it seemed and that I was truly blessed.

Laurie Ritterbach
Pittsburgh, Pennsylvania

**Blood is always needed for emergencies as well as for people who have cancer, blood disorders, sickle-cell anemia, and other such illnesses. Some people need regular blood transfusions to live. To learn how you can donate, visit www.givelife.org.**

**When I was 12, I nearly bled to death** from uterine polyps. Since it took so long for them to realize what was wrong, I needed four units of blood—about half the blood I should have had in my system—to pull through. If four people had not donated their blood, I wouldn't have lived to be 13. Today I am 28, and while I cannot donate blood myself, volunteering with the Long Island Blood Services is a way to give back. I believe that making donors as comfortable as possible now might keep them donating later.

Rebecca Gillman
East Meadow, New York

**I volunteer as a tribute** to my grandmother. She loved to volunteer! She would dress up like a clown with a wig and a big nose and go to the hospital to make the kids there laugh. She passed away last June. I wanted to keep her spirit alive, and volunteering really helped me cope with her death.

Heather Alexakis
Forest Hills, New York

**Before my husband passed away,** I was in an intense caregiving situation. After he died, I missed the feeling that someone needed me. I really needed a mission, but I did not know what I could contribute—I am a 60-year-old woman! One night I saw a news piece about a project where they needed people to bag groceries for AIDS patients, and a light went on. I thought, "That's something I can do; I can bag groceries." I've been volunteering there ever since.

Carol Rehder
Nashville, Tennessee

**Daily, I work toward the vision** that I see articulated in my faith and within my religious tradition, and service is an integral part of that. Woven throughout the Bible are stories of God siding with the poor and caring for them. Matthew 25 discusses how our actions toward "the least of these" are, in effect, our actions toward Jesus. It ought to be our priority to care for those on the margins and those who are most vulnerable.

Rev. Amanda Hendler-Voss
Atlanta, Georgia

**Ever since I can remember,** my mother, Judith Ortiz, instilled in me the love for volunteer work. She belonged to the steering committee for a drug rehab house in Puerto Rico called Hogares Crea. I was so little they called me the mascot of the committee. There I learned the importance of giving and that everyone deserves a second chance. Today, my goal is to pass that torch to my son, because there is no greater heart than the heart of a volunteer.

Philip Alequin
Atlanta, Georgia

**I have been participating in community service** my whole life. I wanted an opportunity to become more deeply involved in local community action. I eventually joined with others in Philadelphia to start Empty the Shelters, an all-volunteer student- and youth-run organization committed to fighting poverty and other forms of oppression through fundamental social change. We created a new approach that wove together service, advocacy work, and direct education. But I realized that some of what we were doing was being fueled by anger and frustration. I knew that we needed to find something to help us cope with the daily struggles we faced, or else we would burn out.

So I connected with two mentors, David and Jennifer Sawyer, who were working to develop a culture of national service. I saw a sense of calm and peace in them that I felt we needed. Grounding myself in spiritual life on a daily basis has helped me to become more aware of the work that most needs doing in the world.

One thing all faith traditions have in common is that being truly serious about having a spiritual life takes discipline. My journey with a spiritual life led me to start stone circles (www.stonecircles.org). Our mission is to sustain activists and strengthen the work of justice through spiritual practice and principles. We are here to share how our spiritual paths and faith traditions can strengthen our work in the world. We recognize that we hold the keys to our own survival and our collective liberation.

Claudia Horwitz
Durham, North Carolina

**In her mid-70s,** my mother-in-law, Billie Brazill, began an unbelievable program for the Pass It Along organization. Raising a large family—she had eight children—meant she was constantly preparing meals, and Billie decided that this was a skill that could be used to benefit others. She decided to take some of her favorite recipes, as well as some new ones, and begin the program affectionately known as Ma's Meals. The family was all behind her, for we all strongly believe in "giving back" in some way. We also benefited as tasters of her sumptuous recipes.

Billie not only created or learned the recipes, she shopped for the ingredients and brought all the goods and utensils that were needed to Sparta, New Jersey, a 90-minute drive from her home, where the cooking would take place. She then taught her recipes to a group of women. These recipes were not run-of-the-mill meals: They consisted of beef tenderloin, pecan-crusted tilapia, extraordinary chicken dishes, and many others (hence our willingness to be taste-testers). Once the meals were prepared, the group would package them individually so that they could be delivered to people in need.

The impact of my mother-in-law's actions touched not only the recipients of her beautiful meals, but also future generations—her children, grandchildren, and great-grandchildren.

Cathy
Sparta, New Jersey

"It's time for greatness—not for greed. It's time for idealism—not ideology. It is a time not just for compassionate words, but compassionate action.
Marian Wright Edelman

**My family and I** have made sacrifices to make volunteer work a priority. In the middle of chairing a large fund-raiser for Children's Healthcare of Atlanta, I worried that I was taking too much time away from my family. Then one night, my four-year-old daughter put on what she calls her "mommy clothes" (a skirt and turtleneck sweater), filled her butterfly backpack with paper and crayons, and told me she was going to a meeting for the "lovey hospital." That inspired me. My children inspire me, knowing they will, in turn, be inspired by the volunteer work they see me do. Ultimately, the act of volunteering has become for me the greatest inspiration of all. When you experience the joy of giving selflessly for others, you want to give again and again.

Deborah P. Miller
Atlanta, Georgia

> "Even if you are on the right track, you'll get run over if you just sit there."
>
> Will Rogers

**My pivotal inspirational experience** came in 1997. I had lost my home, belongings, and money, and my ex-husband had taken custody of two of my sons. I went home to Mexico to stay with my mother. I really thought that the best part of my life was over. Boy was I wrong!

I got to see real poverty in Mexico, and I ended up translating for missionaries. It helped me not to dwell on my problems and instead thank God for His blessings. I ended up helping start a school and a church. Most of all, it helped me see all the blessings around me, and I was able to recover.

Cianna Oliver
Ensenada, Mexico

## Quotes That Inspire

**Martin Luther King Jr.'s quote,** "Life's most urgent question is 'What are you doing for others?'" is such an important question. When I read it, I immediately began looking for ways I could better my community.

Fred Northup Jr.
Seattle, Washington

**"It doesn't matter who** you are underneath; it's what you do that defines you." Volunteering is the "doing" that defines the good inside of us.

Robert Maucher Jr.
Pleasant Valley, New York

**"Even though I am one person,** I can help hundreds." That quote motivates me.

Olivia Hewson
Dover, New Hampshire

**I want to be a thermostat** and not a thermometer! I want to make a change and not just go with the flow.

Meliana Utama
Woodside, New York

## Quotes That Inspire: Editor's Picks

"I slept and dreamt that life was joy. I awoke and saw that life was service. I acted and behold, service was joy."

Rabindranath Tagore

"Never doubt that a small group of thoughtful, devoted citizens can change the world; indeed, it is the only thing that has."

Margaret Mead

"Everyone thinks of changing the world, but no one thinks of changing himself."

Leo Tolstoy

"The world is a dangerous place, not because of those who do evil, but because of those who look on and do nothing."

Albert Einstein

"Until the great mass of the people shall be filled with the sense of responsibility for each other's welfare, social justice can never be attained."

Helen Keller

"You may encounter many defeats, but you must not be defeated. In fact, it may be necessary to encounter the defeats so you can know who you are, what you can rise from, how you can still come out of it."

Maya Angelou

"People may doubt what you say, but they will believe what you do."

Lewis Cass

"I have one life and one chance to make it count for something … I am free to choose what that something is, and the something I've chosen is my faith. Now, my faith goes beyond theology and religion and requires considerable work and effort. My faith demands—this is not optional—my faith demands that I do whatever I can, wherever I am, whenever I can, for as long as I can with whatever I have, to try to make a difference."

Jimmy Carter

## Voices of Change:
## Shareef Cousin

I WAS SENTENCED TO DEATH WHEN I was 16 years old for a murder I didn't commit. I was on death row for five years, spending 23 hours a day in my cell.

At 16, you don't think about fighting for your life, especially for a crime you didn't commit. I thought about how I would never get a chance to graduate high school. I contemplated suicide a few times. I prayed a lot. I cried a lot. And I studied a lot. I always had a desire for education. My lawyers sent me English, math, and science books. I received my GED, and then started college correspondence courses, all at my lawyer's expense.

Once you accept that you are going to die, you learn to find the little things that you can enjoy in each moment. For me it was education. I started helping other inmates with their cases. I never judged people or their situations. I just wanted to help people because someone helped me. Some guys in prison would tell me, "Man, you're wasting your time. That dude doesn't appreciate what you're doing for him." But I was like, "It's not whether he appreciates it. It's about me. I feel good helping him." People helping me steered my path.

Had people not helped me, I'd probably be executed or still on death row. Since my release, I've started work at the Southern Center for Human Rights. I'm now a program organizer for the center's Fairness for Prisoners' Families program. I want to be a trial attorney. I'll be going to Morehouse College in the fall and working full-time.

I do volunteer service too, at a place that provides food and clothes for homeless people. I help feed them, and sometimes I go to Sunday night service and experience fellowship with them.

Being on death row makes you face the fact that, when we die, we all want to know that we've made some sort of contribution to society, however small it may be. And your small bit of help may be large to someone else. What's small to us might make a world of difference to someone else. I wouldn't be here today if people didn't help me. I'm in debt not only to those people but to everyone who does that type of work.

*In 1995, at the age of 16, Shareef Cousin was sentenced to death in Louisiana for a murder he didn't commit. Five years later, the Louisiana Supreme Court overturned his conviction because of improperly withheld evidence. Since his release, Cousin has worked with prisoners' families at the Southern Center for Human Rights in Atlanta.*

# BE THE CHANGE!

## Books That Inspire

*The Measure of Our Success: A Letter to My Children and Yours* by Marian Wright Edelman taught me to extend my hand to those who don't get second chances. Remember the kids who face real monsters every day, the kids whose pictures aren't on anyone's desk. Thinking about those kids keeps me going.

Diamond Leshane
Atlanta, Georgia

*Amazing Grace* by Jonathan Kozol illuminated for me the day-to-day challenges low-income families face in New York City.

Marlo Hyman
New York, New York

*The Power of One* by Bryce Courtenay tells the true story of the struggles of a child in South Africa, and it really motivates me.

Amanda Duntz
Lebanon, Connecticut

**Reading biographies of various leaders** also inspires me. I have recently been reading the biographies of our founding fathers, and continue to be amazed at the faith, foresight, and intellect of those who founded this great nation.

Thomas Lyon
Raleigh, North Carolina

***Soul of a Citizen*** and *The Impossible Will Take a Little While* by Paul Rogat Loeb give clear, concrete examples of people who are making a difference. They give me hope!

Kim Smith
Portland, Oregon

***The Legacy of Luna*** by Julia Butterfly Hill. Anyone who stands up for what they believe in is inspiring, and Julia Butterfly Hill lived in a tree for two years regardless of what she had to go through.

Teri Harp
El Cajon, California

*War Talk* by Arundhati Roy, *Other People's Children* by Lisa Delpit, *ZenZele: A Letter for My Daughter* by J. Nozipo Maraire, *Sister Outsider* by Audre Lorde, and everything by Nikki Giovanni.

Cindy Lutenbacher
Atlanta, Georgia

*Night* by Elie Wiesel, about a boy in the Holocaust, made me want to change the world. I realized how bad the world can get, and that people could have helped but didn't want to get involved. I don't want to be someone who waits until it gets to a critical point to really start doing something about it.

Brittney Lemley
Reno, Nevada

## Books That Inspire: Editor's Picks

Fiction

*The Adventures of Huckleberry Finn* by Mark Twain
*All the King's Men* by Robert Penn Warren
*Invisible Man* by Ralph Ellison
*A Lesson Before Dying* by Ernest J. Gaines
*Their Eyes Were Watching God* by Zora Neale Hurston
*A Room of One's Own* by Virginia Woolf
*To Kill a Mockingbird* by Harper Lee
*The God of Small Things* by Arundhati Roy
*For Whom the Bell Tolls* by Ernest Hemingway
Any book by Leo Tolstoy

Nonfiction

*Profiles in Courage* by John F. Kennedy
*The Call of Stories* and *The Call of Service* by Robert Coles
*Letter from Birmingham Jail* by Martin Luther King Jr.
*On Self-Reliance* by Ralph Waldo Emerson
Abraham Lincoln's second inaugural address and
   Gettysburg address

## Editor's Picks: Children's Books

The spirit of giving often is instilled at a very young age, and children's books can provide a lifelong reservoir of inspiration. Whether you are young or old, these timeless stories will touch you.

*Anansi the Spider: A Tale from the Ashanti* by Gerald McDermott
*Abiyoyo* by Pete Seeger, illustrated by Michael Hays
*A Chair for My Mother* by Vera B. Williams
*A Tree Is Nice* by Janice May Udry, illustrated by Marc Simont
*The Carrot Seed* by Ruth Krauss
*Charlotte's Web* by E. B. White, illustrated by Garth Williams
*The Chronicles of Narnia* by C. S. Lewis
*Dr. White* by Jane Goodall, illustrated by Julie Litty
*Frog and Toad Together* by Arnold Lobel
*The Giving Tree* by Shel Silverstein
*Horton Hears A Who!* by Dr. Seuss
*It Could Always Be Worse* by Margot Zemach
*The Little Engine That Could* by Watty Piper
*Miss Fannie's Hat* by Jan Karon, illustrated by Toni Goffe
*Miss Rumphius* by Barbara Clooney
*Mr. Rabbit and the Lovely Present* by Charlotte Zolotow,
  illustrated by Maurice Sendak
*Old Turtle* by Douglas Wood, illustrated by Cheng-Khee Chee
*On the Day You Were Born* by Debra Frasier

## Voices of Change: Helene Gayle

I have always believed that teachers play a critical role in shaping an individual's path. My path towards trying to affect social change did not begin in a classroom, though. Neither were my first educators trained classroom teachers. I got my first lessons from Jacob and Marietta Gayle, my parents, who instilled in me the belief that working to bring about positive social change was one's highest calling. I was fortunate to have grown up in a family that placed a high value on education, thinking and speaking for myself, and giving back to society. I was also shaped by growing up at a point in history when the hotly debated issues of our time were civil rights, anti-apartheid, women's rights, struggles for liberation from colonialism, and the Vietnam War. This helped develop my desire to be part of something greater than myself and my sense of a collective responsibility for the future of our world.

I went into medicine, and ultimately public health, because I saw these as tools that would enable me to band with others to make concrete contributions to addressing social inequity for large numbers of people around the world. Inequities in health often have as much to do with underlying social and economic injustice as they do with any specific cause of illness. Having a sustained impact on health issues of people living in poverty requires tackling the root causes of vulnerability to disease such as lack of education, gender inequity, malnutrition, unsafe water, and poor sanitation.

Becoming a doctor seemed like a concrete way to make a positive contribution to society and help address one of the great areas of social inequity—the unequal health status between the haves and have-nots in our country and around the world. So I entered medical school with the view that medicine should be a tool to make a difference in peoples' lives and address social injustice. While in medical school, I began to learn more about public health and thought it might be a good way to combine my training as a doctor with my interest in addressing health issues at a broader level.

I had one of those lightning-bolt moments when I heard a commencement speech at my younger brother's graduation ceremony by D. A. Henderson, one of the leaders of the worldwide campaign to eradicate smallpox. I was simply awed by the audacity of the effort he described. Using the tools of public health, he and people like him around the world took on smallpox—a disease that is estimated to have taken over 500 million lives since the time of the Pharaohs—and wiped it from the face of the earth.

I realized right then that I would use my career to improve the health of people around the world. Interestingly, I have spent much of my professional life working on HIV and AIDS. I ended up drawn to working on HIV because of the societal imperative that it poses.

Communities and nations that have been successful in slowing the spread of HIV have done so by changing the way people view and relate to each other. Making a difference in the fight against HIV, a disease that disproportionately affects the poor and the socially marginalized, means affirming that all life matters and has equal value whether you are an injecting drug user in Eastern Europe, a gay man in North America, or a woman engaged in commercial sex in Africa or Asia.

My journey that began at my father's beauty and barber supply store in the heart of Buffalo's black neighborhood has taken me through interesting turns. Have I come full circle? In many ways I have. I can't imagine a better way to use what I have learned in my years in public health to now work to address the very issues that brought me to medicine and public health to begin with. Ending poverty is, after all, the ultimate way to save lives.

*Dr. Helene Gayle is the CEO of CARE, an organization that tackles underlying causes of poverty so that people can become self-sufficient. Women are at the heart of CARE's community-based efforts to improve basic education, prevent the spread of HIV, increase access to clean water and sanitation, expand economic opportunity, and protect natural resources. CARE also delivers emergency aid to survivors of war and natural disasters, and helps people rebuild their lives. To learn more about this organization, visit www.care.org.*

# REFLECTIONS

M Y WORK WITH HANDS ON NETWORK is to help people begin their service journey. I have led orientations for thousands of individuals who have decided to take the first step to make a difference. Their specific reasons for wanting to serve are as varied as they are. But common themes emerge at every orientation: "I want to do something that is larger than myself, to make the community better, to find something that is truly meaningful in my life." Or, "I want to get to know others in the community who share my values for giving back. I want to feel like I am a part of the community."

Sometimes, they are motivated by a specific event. When I talk to volunteers responding in the wake of 2005's Hurricane Katrina, they often say things like, "I just knew I had to be a part of this." When they saw images of people suffering, they felt that they must act. Many acted on impulse, driving hundreds or thousands of miles into an unknown situation to find a way to serve. Everyone that I have spoken with has expressed passion and gratitude that they took that first step. While you may begin with uncertainty, you will find confidence and fulfillment as you proceed. As one volunteer once said to me, "I am always glad I came."

M.N.

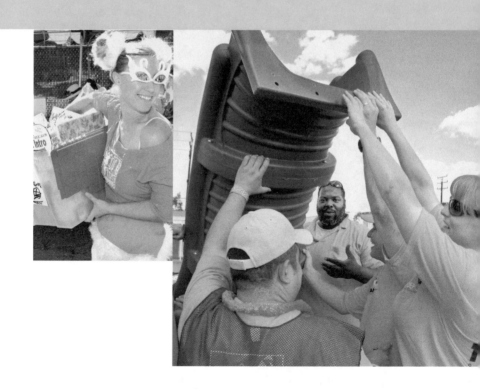

# CHAPTER 2

## Words from the wise
### TIPS TO CONSIDER WHEN DIVING IN

IN A WORLD OF ENORMOUS NEEDS and some seemingly insurmountable problems, how do we find our own way to make a difference? One of the stories in this chapter recalls a conversation with famed conservationist and scientist Jane Goodall, in which she answers this question by saying, "Just find your piece of it."

Just find your piece—find the place where your gifts and the world's needs are well matched. Advice on how to begin and how to find your service calling varies—some advise to go slow, take small bites, evaluate your commitment and interests, and find an organization that suits you. Others encourage diving in— just do it and work out the details later. Whatever course seems right for you, the service journey begins with the first step. Don't let apathy, fear, or uncertainty become obstacles. Goethe said it well: "Whatever you can do, or dream you can, begin it. Boldness has genius, power, and magic in it."

In my years of working with volunteers, one thing is clear to me: there is a role for everyone who wants to make a difference. Each of us has talents, passions, and interests that can be applied to help others. Whether you like to work out front or behind the scenes, directly with people, or doing administrative tasks—there are innumerable ways that you can contribute. You can "connect the dots" of your life—your professional skill, your hobbies and passions, your relationships, your wealth—and create a landscape of change.

In preparing for a service journey, it is important to equip yourself with fundamental values that will serve you well—no matter the effort. Bring humility, authenticity, perseverance, and commitment to see your work through. Bring respect and tolerance for those you are serving and the openness to learn from others and find discoveries in the unexpected. And don't forget to bring a healthy dose of humor to keep it all in perspective and sustain yourself through trials and challenges.

Service can be as large as starting an initiative to build wheelchair ramps for people with disabilities, as focused as signing for the deaf one evening a week, or as simple as contributing to a community garden. Each of these initiatives begins with these questions: How can I help? What's my piece of it? The following stories will help you find your own way to begin.

**Jane Goodall, the renowned primatologist,** gave me some fantastic advice once. I went to see her when I was attending college and completely overwhelmed by all of the world's problems. I wanted to do something about them, but what? I asked her what I could do and she replied: "Just find your piece of it." I think that's excellent advice. Simply narrow the world's problems down to what you can best identify with and work on that one problem. A perfect example of that is my friend who grew up in the welfare system. These days she focuses on welfare issues. She found her piece of it!

Denise Riebman
Boston, Massachusetts

**The best way to inspire kids** is to make the result you want from them appear very real to them. I once worked as a Big Brother, and my little brother was nine. One day he shared with me that he had been working as a delivery boy for the drug dealers in his neighborhood. Instead of yelling at him, I tried to show him how much better his life could be if he stayed off that path.

I asked him to think about his father (who was in prison), and I asked him if he wanted to spend time in prison. He said no. Then I told him to look at me, someone who had come over from a different country to enjoy a good life in the United States. I asked him what kind of life he would rather have. Once I did that, I told him that keeping clean, working hard, and staying away from drugs could keep him out of prison and in a good life. I urged him to tell his mother about what he'd been doing, and to stop delivering drugs. He eventually did, and his mother moved him out of that neighborhood. If I had just lectured him that drugs were bad, he might not have understood.

Erastus Mong'are
Newark, Delaware

Big Brothers Big Sisters is the oldest and largest youth mentoring organization in the United States. It has been the leader in one-to-one youth service for more than a century, developing positive relationships that have a direct and lasting impact on the lives of young people. Big Brothers Big Sisters serves children ages six through 18 in communities across the country. For more information, log on to www.bbbs.org.

**When you're working** with less fortunate people, your job is not to judge how they got there. You have no idea what that person's life is like. Judging someone for their current life condition is as rude and wrong as walking up to someone in a restaurant and saying, "You need to lose 10 pounds. You shouldn't be eating that for lunch!"

Liz McAllister
Chicago, Illinois

**Start in a small,** supportive role in an organization before making a full commitment. It's not just smarter for you, but it might save that organization time and money. Organizations all have their own unique personalities and dynamics. Even if the organization's vision and mission are compatible with your values, look carefully. Interviewing, performing background checks, and training volunteers takes the organization time and energy. For them, there is nothing worse than having someone decide, after they have been oriented and placed in a position, that "this isn't what I thought it would be."

Penny Townsend-Quill
Rochester, New York

To find nonpartisan information on elected officials' voting records and candidates' positions see www.vote-smart.org.

**If you never have done any community service,** try volunteering for a political campaign. You will meet people from all walks of life who share your passion. It's also a great starter opportunity since there is a limited time frame. You know when it begins and ends so you won't ever get stuck in it.

Sara Needleman-Carlton
Seattle, Washington

**If you don't go into it with the proper perspective,** volunteering with seniors can be very depressing. Focus on your efforts and not on the problems that come with aging and with loneliness. You can't change the aging process, but you *can* make the lives of some people better. Whatever time you dedicate to doing that is time that will make it better for these folks.

Bob Young
Charlotte, North Carolina

**San Francisco has one of the highest** independent senior populations in the nation. But they're not really connected with a community, and they don't really know what's out there in regard to things like Medicare and Social Security. So we run a Senior Survival School. We give them books in which they can look up their own benefits and translate them into their native languages. It makes them more independent and proud. People who were living in one tiny little room before coming to our school are now living in two-bedroom apartments. A little knowledge and confidence, and these seniors are improving the quality of their own lives. Best of all, they're doing it themselves!

Amihan Makayahn
San Francisco, California

**Volunteer. Just do it.** It is like explaining the taste of barbecue to someone who has never tasted it. The experience will explain it better than I ever could.

Joe Mullin
Round Rock, Texas

Senior Survival School is a program that teaches seniors and people with disabilities about the resources in their communities. The mission of Senior Survival School is to provide seniors of all ages, languages, income levels, and health levels with the information, understanding, and contacts necessary to empower and motivate them, increase their independence, enhance the quality of their lives, and ensure their access to health, housing, transit and other support services. Visit www.senior-survivalschool.org to learn more.

**One of the best, easiest,** and most rewarding volunteer activities you can try is being an official hugger for the Special Olympics. All you have to do is stand there at the end of the race, and hug them for finishing. Everybody's a winner. It's amazing!

Joel Kunkler
Rochester, New York

Special Olympics is an international nonprofit organization dedicated to empowering individuals with intellectual disabilities to become physically fit, productive, and respected members of society through sports training and competition. Visit www.special olympics.org to learn more.

**One does not have to do something huge** to do something good. You simply have to do something good.

Jenna Citron
Lake Worth, Florida

**You can never forget,** while working with kids, that just by talking about your career, college experience, or internship, you're creating a possibility. You're helping them imagine and put shape to what they might become.

Tripp Singer
New York, New York

**A lot of people don't realize** the variety of opportunities that exist. I've done everything from ushering at an opera to cooking breakfast for families with sick children to selling peanuts for a fund-raiser at a football game. There's a need for fast typists, creative writers, and people who work well with children. Look around for events and find something that speaks to you, something you think you could really excel at.

Heather Leah
Raleigh, North Carolina

## Practical Advice for the Plunge

**As great as it is to volunteer as a family,** never assume you can bring your kids with you when you volunteer. Always check with the agency to be sure it is a child-friendly project or a child-friendly environment. For example, a child may be able to help serve a meal, but not work in the kitchen and cook a meal. So check first, or you risk everyone having to go home.

Cindy Huggett
Raleigh, North Carolina

**Even if you're not a "people person,"** there are plenty of ways to serve your community. You don't need to work with kids or the homeless. There are dogs that need walking, there are office jobs where you can do administrative things. If you like working with gardens, you can do that too. Just you and the plants; you don't need to talk to anyone.

Jeanette Gisbert
New York, New York

**At the heart of volunteering** is the rightful belief that helping others is a good thing. But sometimes, helping others makes their lives worse even while the helper is basking in the warmth of a job seemingly well done. Unfortunately, helping that does not acknowledge and use the gifts of the person being helped may leave the person and the community weaker.

Helping can be a hand reached down from the strong to the weak. Helping can also leave the one helped more dependent and less hopeful. Helping can result in people grateful for someone else's gifts but unsure of their own.

So when does helping help? When does the volunteer's work enable another person or an entire community to become stronger?

One of the founders of community organizing, Saul Alinsky, had an iron rule: "Never do for another what they can do for themselves." He knew the powerful truth that people want to take care of themselves rather than being dependent on or beholden to others, and that each step people take on their own makes them stronger and increases their ability to take the next step forward. John McKnight, a pioneer in building community, says in his article "Why Servanthood Is Bad" that doing for others does not work, but actually undermines them.

Instead, when people appreciate each other's gifts and help each other, they walk away as better people. More important, if the neighborhood where you serve is left with resources the people there control, and if the people are left better organized to confront their problems, the helping hand truly is a helping hand.

Jon Abercrombie
Atlanta, Georgia

**I am a college student studying** computer information systems. I have used the knowledge that I have acquired to build two Web sites for various nonprofits, to build entire databases and troubleshoot a computer lab for Girls Inc., to teach computer classes to at-risk youth in my area, and to write and obtain a grant for a local volunteer organization, Hands On Columbus.

Melissa Chaney
Columbus, Georgia

**I am an artist,** so I volunteer to paint murals on schools for LA Works. I am also a software/Web developer and volunteer for two high schools, teaching Web design. I am also a chef, so I organize volunteers to prepare meals for HIV/AIDS organizations.

Kristen Yolas
Sherman Oaks, California

**I used to be a pro at a local golf course.** Though I've since gone into finance, I still volunteer my time teaching young people to play golf on the weekends. I have enough pointers I can give to youngsters to get them headed in the right direction.

Philip Orons
Kennedy, New York

**Girls Inc. is a national non-profit youth organization dedicated to inspiring all girls to be strong, smart, and bold. With roots dating to 1864, Girls Inc. has provided vital educational programs to millions of American girls, particularly those in high-risk, under-served areas. Today, innovative programs help girls confront subtle societal messages about their value and potential and prepare them to lead successful, independent, and fulfilling lives. For more information, visit www.girlsinc.org.**

## Voices of Change:
## Keith Brooking

"My mother was a great role model for me. She took on foster kids from the time I was a kid, and we had numerous children come through our home. Being very young at the time, I didn't know a lot about life and what it meant to give to others. We were poor and I didn't even know it. We didn't have a lot growing up; it was a struggle to put food on the table and pay bills. But my mom raised these kids and gave them all their needs. I think that's amazing.

Of course, not every story had a great ending. My mom had kids in her home whom she tried her best with, but they were too scarred from their pasts. They would run away, and it would affect our household. They would have to move on. But for every one of those stories, there were four or five really good ones. My mom had a girl in her home for six years whose life was a complete wreck from abuse by her siblings and family. But my mom had a great impact on her life. This girl graduated from high school, got a great job, and moved away. But she eventually came back and got married, and she has her own family now. They have built their own home, and they come by to visit my mom all the time. She and my mom talk on the phone every day.

Now that I am grown, I realize what that's all about. I got into the NFL in 1998, and I always wanted to start a foundation; I wanted to give back to the community. But I didn't want to jump into it immediately. I wanted to do something meaningful. After a few years with the Falcons, I signed a new contract and knew I would be in Atlanta for a while. That's when I decided to start my foundation, which serves foster children. I know about the need for foster parents, and in the position I'm in today, I have the resources to affect a lot of kids in a positive way.

We've done a lot of great things for foster kids in the community, sometimes working with other groups to do so. There's such a need for so many things in our communities. I realize that every person in America is in a different situation, and I'm fortunate that I have the time and resources to help people. But I really believe with my heart that everyone can make a positive impact in some way. Look at my mother. We had very little, but she found something she had a passion for, and she made an impact.

There's something out there for everyone. There's something that's close and dear to you. Try to make an impact in something you have that love for.

*Keith Brooking is a Pro Bowl linebacker for the Atlanta Falcons. He was named the Falcons' Man of the Year in 2002 for his extensive community involvement. He founded the Keith Brooking Children's Foundation in 2003.*

**No skill or passion should sit idly;** every action or hobby can become a conscious or unconscious volunteer event. I love to ride my bicycle, and this summer I am going to Lake Tahoe for a 100-mile ride benefiting the Leukemia & Lymphoma Society. I am volunteering my passion and time, but bringing everyone—including coworkers—along with me.

Lenny Reisner
Brighton, Massachusetts

**I love black-and-white photography,** so now I volunteer to teach a photography class to fifth-graders who attend inner-city schools.

Beth Fenger
Atlanta, Georgia

**Before I started volunteering** for women's health issues, I didn't know that so much of community organizing relies on the accuracy of writing and research. I'm probably not going to be the person tabling or collecting signatures (even though I have done these tasks, sparingly), but I will be there fact-checking, editing, and drafting documents. These are opportunities I hadn't previously considered. But they are just as important.

Lucy Kelly
Whitefish Bay, Wisconsin

"Tell me and I'll forget. Show me and I might remember. Involve me and I'll understand."
Chinese proverb

I **grew up in a privileged environment** where I was fortunate enough to obtain a great education and attend an Ivy League university. I was on track to become a biologist, when something made me stop and think about whether that was what I really wanted. I decided to defer my admission to graduate school for one year and join AmeriCorps. That experience was unlike anything that I had ever experienced in my life. After spending a year working with a diverse group of people in communities with deep needs, I knew that I could not go on to live the rest of my life in a laboratory. I eventually declined my biology graduate program altogether, and I continued to serve with AmeriCorps as a team leader for a second year. I knew I needed to find a way to merge my desire to serve with my desire to further my education. I got my master's degree in public policy and am currently a Ph.D. student. I continue to look for ways to combine my intellectual interests with public service. That's one of the great things about service. You don't have to have any special qualifications or come from a special place. Anyone can use whatever resources or knowledge they have to help others.

Diana Epstein
Berkeley, California

AmeriCorps*VISTA provides full-time members to non-profit, faith-based, and other community organizations, and public agencies to create and expand programs that ultimately bring low-income individuals and communities out of poverty. Through AmeriCorps*VISTA, ordinary people provide extraordinary service in more than 1,200 projects nationwide. To become involved, visit www.americorps.gov/about/programs/vista.asp.

## Making a Difference for Children

*For many people, helping children find their way is at the top of their priority list in serving others. Here are some ideas for making the most of your commitment to children.*

**Spoiling the kids you serve** is not helping them at all. Just because a neighborhood is downtrodden doesn't mean the kids don't deserve the same level of discipline and guidance on how to behave properly.

Malikah Berry
Atlanta, Georgia

**Don't be afraid to share yourself.** I was working with kids who were going through tough times, and they would ask me, "So what's *your* story?" I initially felt that unless I could say that one of my parents was a drug addict or that I too had been in foster care, they wouldn't take me seriously. But they just wanted to know what my day-to-day life was like, what my job was like, and whether I had any kids.

Marlo Hyman
New York, New York

**Realize that other people** are just as worthy of respect as you are, even people you are helping. I was volunteering in a special education classroom, and one of my younger students, Mallory, kept telling me that she had already done a work sheet that I was forcing her to do. Her teacher had told me otherwise, so I didn't listen, but she raised her voice and told me, "Just because you're older than me doesn't mean you know everything. Sometimes you need to listen to children because they know things you don't."

As it turns out, Mallory *had* done the work sheet, and both the teacher and I were wrong. I learned a great lesson that day, and I have always admired Mallory for teaching it to me. After that incident, I have always credited every being with an adequate amount of respect.

Nausheen Shaikh
Granger, Indiana

**Even when you're being pushed away,** never go away. When I was a mentor, my mentee tried to shock me. She would get into trouble; she would run away. But I never abandoned her. I knew it was important for me to stick it out.

Dawn Balzarano
Sacramento, California

## Ideas for Finding Your Piece of It

**Tell your story.** It can take your project or cause to places you have never imagined. As an AmeriCorps*VISTA volunteer, I organized a yard cleanup for a local family in which two members had disabilities. A newspaper article was run on this family, and the next thing I knew, I was in front of our local Community Development Corporation asking for $40,000 to renovate their home to make it wheelchair-accessible. Our sincere expression of need took this family from being prisoners in their home to independence.

Ericka Zdenek
Tallahassee, Florida

**I never considered myself enough** of an expert in any sport to teach young kids how to do it. But the first year I signed my son up for baseball and started going to the games, I realized that the guys who were coaching didn't know any more than I did. But they were willing to take the time and the effort to give the kids an outlet to play. Now my main volunteer activity is coaching Little League baseball and soccer.

Rorry Hollenbeck
Jamestown, New York

**Connect the dots in your life.** That's where you can do the most powerful work. I spent decades in the business world and when I finally retired, I got bored. So I went back to one of my earlier passions: music. What started as a substitute position ended up as a full-time job teaching music to kids.

At the same time I began volunteering with the Make-A-Wish Foundation. I was traveling overseas a lot for this organization, and one day it hit me: Why not take my students to play concerts for Make-A-Wish fund-raisers? The first time I wanted to bring our band with me to Europe, people were saying, "What are you, nuts?" These days I'm taking 70 kids at a time. My business background helped make a lot of these trips possible, and now we have major sponsors and are requested to play at many events. When I brought together my business, music, and volunteer work, everything clicked.

Danny Lieberman
Fort Lauderdale, Florida

**You can really find almost anything** if you just put the word out. I basically operate like a distribution center, finding out what poor and immigrant families in the neighborhood need and working with the local social service agency to find those things. For example, I know kids in a housing development who had never, ever had a Christmas tree, so I called around and found a friend who had a truly beautiful artificial tree—it had lights and everything—and she was throwing it out, even though there was nothing wrong with it. I picked it up from her and took it to that family. The children were really excited.

Janet Lund
Minneapolis, Minnesota

# Words from the Wise

**In serving, you have to recognize** your place in the process. You may not be the visionary who's standing in front of thousands, but that's OK; the envelope stuffers are just as important. Every single little task is necessary to make change happen.

Genora Crooke
Atlanta, Georgia

**Leave your ego at the door.** Even if you're a powerful person in your professional life, you may have to sit back and let someone else tell you what to do.

Kim Ross
Atlanta, Georgia

**The first time I volunteered,** I remember it was harder work than I expected. People tend to discount volunteering as easy work, but it can be like moving out of a house. It seems easy, but the details are endless, the workload is heavy, *and* you're on a timeline.

Robert Poitras
Chapel Hill, North Carolina

## Voices of Change: Richard Goldsmith

I always wanted to improve the lives of kids, but with my travel schedule, I knew I couldn't be a Little League coach or a mentor. So a group of friends and I identified one of the neediest schools in Atlanta and made an appointment with the principal. We sat down with him and found out what his needs were. We told him we couldn't help out financially, but we had manpower. He told us they needed tutors and asked us what we could manage. We said we could commit some people to come in from 10 a.m. to noon on a Saturday to tutor. He asked us when we could start, and we looked at each other and said, "How about next Saturday?"

That was it! Back then, we only had about 20 volunteers for Hands On Atlanta, none of whom had educational experience. But that didn't stop us. We did not have a program of any kind in place; we just dove in and created it as we went along. Since then, our Saturday morning initiative has grown into a highly organized, nationally replicated program called the Discovery Program, involving thousands of children and tutors. We have been volunteering with this program and school for more than a decade, and a number of the children we began tutoring now return as volunteers.

I learned three valuable lessons about starting a successful community service project:

1. Dive in headfirst. If you want to help, just go out there and find out what the community's needs are. Then get started and worry about the details later.

2. Make sure you create a program you can commit to and you know others can commit to. I firmly believe that one of the reasons we have been so successful and that this project has lasted so long is because we have restricted the time commitment to two hours. A time commitment from 10 a.m. to noon on Saturdays can fit easily into the busiest of schedules.

3. Be organized and you will keep your volunteers. We are structured to the point of being neurotic. We are such a well-oiled machine that I know I can keep my promise when I tell volunteers to show up at 10 a.m. and they definitely will be on their way home by 12:05 p.m.

*Richard Goldsmith began recruiting volunteers as tutors and mentors for the children at one of the neediest elementary schools in Fulton County, Georgia, more than 15 years ago through Hands On Atlanta. Since then, his Saturday morning initiative has grown into a highly organized, nationally replicated program called the Discovery Program. This program is a grassroots community approach to assist youth, requiring a relatively low level of financial assistance but great amounts of human energy and concern.*

## Voices of Change:
## Bill Novelli

"

I have a deep interest in making a contribution to solving major social problems and creating positive social change. In fact, I have a favorite saying: 'Problems worthy of attack prove their worth by attacking back.' We need to address the big, tough issues that do 'attack back,' which is what makes them so tough to solve in the first place.

I didn't start my career with such lofty aims. My goal after college was to get a good job at a big company that offered health benefits and the chance to climb the rungs of the corporate ladder. My first job was in consumer marketing at Unilever, working with packaged food and home goods. I left Unilever to go to what was then a hot New York ad agency, Wells Rich Green. I was climbing the ladder, but in spite of my progress, I felt that something was missing. I just didn't think the packaged-goods marketing and advertising game was enough for me. I wanted something that I vaguely thought of as more socially relevant.

I was determined to change course. As I began to explore how and where, I was assigned a new client, the Public Broadcasting Service. One of my first tasks was to attend a press conference that featured Joan Ganz Cooney, one of the creators of *Sesame Street*. I was fascinated by Cooney and by the *Sesame Street* approach to learning. The thought struck me that marketing tools and practices could be applied to ideas, issues, and causes just as effectively as to the laundry detergents, toothpastes, and pet foods I had been promoting. This was relevant, I thought, and socially important. I wanted to try it, but how could I go about making it into a career?

The answer came when I learned that the Peace Corps wanted to 'reposition' itself, to attract more volunteers with job experience and work skills that were in demand among developing countries. They were looking for a marketing person, and I landed the job. I was on my way to realizing my new ambition.

Jack Porter, my boss at the Peace Corps, had also left a commercial marketing career to work for the Peace Corps, and he, too, was intrigued with the idea of marketing ideas and causes. We decided to start a firm just for this purpose, Porter Novelli, dedicated to applying marketing to health and social issues. Our first major assignment was to help the newly instituted National High Blood Pressure Education Program (considered perhaps the most successful national health education program in U.S. history) reach out to the medical profession and the public about the lifesaving advantages of treating high blood pressure.

In time, Porter Novelli became involved in many health and social issues, including environmental protection, cancer detection and control, and reproductive health and infant survival in developing countries. We also brought in commercial clients, which helped us grow, but social issues and ideas were what made me eager to go to work each day. I wanted more than ever to focus there. So I 'retired' from Porter Novelli, at the age of 49, to pursue a full-time career in public service. Porter Novelli continued to grow, and today it is a large, international public relations agency and part of the Omnicom Group, a global marketing communications corporation.

I went to CARE, the world's largest private international relief and development organization. I had previously served on CARE's board of directors, and I was familiar with the agency's mission and the work it did in developing countries. CARE's management and staff wanted to make a difference in the world, which they did through development programs as well as by managing refugee camps, helping victims of natural disasters, and risking their lives in dangerous settings.

After four and a half years at CARE, which included work on the Somalia and Rwanda crises, my next role in public service was as a founder and president of the Campaign for Tobacco-Free Kids—'a tobacco institute for the good guys.' The tobacco war is far from over, but the Campaign for Tobacco-Free Kids and others are working hard, and things are changing for the better.

When I was appointed chief executive of AARP in mid-2001, I felt as if my whole career had been preparation for this one job. I believe deeply in AARP's mission of enhancing our lives as we age. It speaks to all generations, those that are younger as well as those that are over 50. At AARP, we are at the forefront of one of the most important societal changes of all time—the aging of America and the world. This is an exciting opportunity to influence events and social change in the unfolding drama of an aging population. I guess you could say that I'm one of those lucky people who chased a dream and caught it. I found my perfect opportunity to make a difference—to help combat those 'problems worthy of attack that prove their worth by attacking back.'

*Bill Novelli is the CEO of the American Association of Retired Persons (AARP). Each year, AARP honors the legacy of its founder, Dr. Ethel Percy Andrus, with the AARP Andrus Award for Community Service, AARP's most prestigious and visible volunteer award. If you know of an AARP volunteer or AARP member who has made a significant contribution to his or her community, consider honoring that service by nominating them at www.aarp.org/volunteer.*

# REFLECTIONS

IN 1987, A GROUP OF NEW YORKERS GOT TOGETHER and started to organize a new way for people to serve their community. They started organizing group projects on weekends and in evenings to accommodate the schedules of busy professionals. They made it easy to say yes by requiring no long-term commitment, just an invitation to a meaningful, hands-on project that left participants feeling like they had made a small but real difference. They called their effort New York Cares. Soon, some of their friends moved to new cities and brought the idea and organizing principles to Atlanta, Washington, D.C., and Chicago. Within a few years, thousands of people were working in communities doing dozens of service projects every month. Almost 20 years later, this movement has transformed itself into Hands On Network. It has extended to almost 65 communities, and in 2005, more than 50,000 projects were completed. Every day, Hands On volunteers build wheelchair ramps, perform extreme makeovers of public schools, tutor children, and renovate houses.

No matter what your skills or talents may be, no matter how much time you may have, there is work to be done. Be aware that you are most powerful when working *with* someone; recognize the powerful bonds of reciprocity.

M.N.

# CHAPTER 3

# Some other benefits of service
## SELFISH REASONS TO BE SELFLESS

PERHAPS THE MOST FUNDAMENTAL LESSON of serving others is that it is a reciprocal experience. You might begin by thinking that you are doing something for others—and you are—but you will invariably find that you are getting a lot out of it too. It is trite, but true, that in reaching out to serve others, you will often get more out of the experience than you give.

The stories in this chapter show us the magical and sometimes unexpected gifts of service. We see that when we start out to make a difference in someone else's life, we inevitably change our own.

When we reach out in service, we also reach out to new friends—those we are serving and those that we serve alongside. We may even find romantic connections—can you think of a better way to meet someone who is compassionate, community-minded, and shares your values? In reaching out, we cultivate roots in our community and create the vital "stickiness" that binds us to our neighbors far and near. We create the relationships that both lend perspective and sustain us during our own times of difficulty.

And there are myriad practical reasons to serve and work for change. As a volunteer, you can take on unlimited leadership challenges and exercise aspects of your intellect and skills that you might not have an opportunity to apply anywhere else. You can develop new skills—from practicing a second language to learning new computer programs. If you want to become a chef, how about experimenting by cooking at a local shelter? You might start out as a volunteer tutor and discover that your true calling is to be a teacher. Or perhaps you will learn through your volunteer internship at the public defender's office that you really don't want to be a lawyer after all. I have known dozens of people who started out as volunteers and ended up as professional staff—they found their callings, and the organizations where they were working found passionate, committed employees who understood the work.

As we discover the fundamental rewards of service, we will rediscover ourselves, learning lessons of patience and courage that will help us overcome our fears and face the world bravely. As contributor Beth Senko says, "Volunteering gives you confidence and superhuman strength. I am now officially a superhero!" The people you will meet in this chapter have taken that voyage of discovery, and the riches they have reaped can be yours as well.

**Service is a chance for me** to be more than my deafness. Growing up, it was always, "There goes Michael, the deaf guy." But now I've done so much else that people don't identify me that way. I'm a youth adviser, I like to go rock climbing, and I'm weird! People now say, "There goes Michael, he's the guy who helps us do this or that."

Michael Agyin
Los Angeles, California

**Volunteering allows me to feel less helpless.** There are so many things going on in the world that are out of my control. I'd rather be active about them than sit here and whine and complain. When I was a college freshman, the war was going on in Kosovo. I remember watching the news and feeling so disgusted with humanity. I knew there had to be *something* I could do. So I started a fund-raising campaign on my campus. Volunteering in Kosovo wasn't an option at that time, but I could at least raise money to help support the programs going on over there.

Rachel Mahoney
Astoria, New York

"The more you lose yourself in something bigger than yourself, the more energy you will have."

Dr. Norman Vincent Peale

**Effective volunteering is like living** a healthy lifestyle. If you stick with it, you will eventually see results. When I first started volunteering at a transitional home, I was the only person who showed up. So I became the coordinator and stuck with it. Two years later, we now have 20 regular volunteers.

Ann Gregg
Boston, Massachusetts

## Service and Your Health

**When we take action to make** our mark in the world, we also learn how to take control. We affirm our own power in the world, defeating the sense of impotence that can render us frustrated and depressed. We gain new perspectives and develop capacities for empathy, inspiration, or courage that help bolster and guide us in overcoming our own obstacles. By putting our will and our abilities into service we redefine ourselves—overcoming our fears, limitations, or disabilities and turning them into assets.

I recommend incorporating some kind of service work into your weekly or monthly routine. Doing service work puts the needs of others ahead of your own, and that does good both for you and the people you're helping … whatever form your service work takes, once you take that first step you'll find it will quickly become one of your more rewarding healthy habits.

Andrew Weil, M.D.
Vail, Arizona

*Andrew Weil, M.D., is a world-famous doctor and author, offering counsel on integrating holistic and scientific medicine.*

**Volunteering is a lot like working out.** You may dread the initial going-to-the-gym phase, but if you focus on how good you'll feel afterward, it's way easier to stay motivated. If I am not sure I'm going to be able to make myself get up and volunteer, I think of how great I will feel after I do. Works every time.

Melissa Bieri
New York, New York

**Originally I became a volunteer** in the hopes of making new friends. Then, in November 2001, I was laid off from my job. The next day I was scheduled to work at a volunteer project. I was still emotional from having been told my position was eliminated and that I needed to clean out my desk. I couldn't stop crying, and I was worried about how I would pay the bills.

The project I signed up for involved working with children who were autistic or had physical disabilities. After spending the morning with several kids, I went home and cried for a whole different reason. I asked myself, "What am I afraid of? Why should I worry? I have two arms, two legs, and an education, and I can feed and dress myself." I knew I had nothing to worry about and that I would be OK. That was when I realized I wasn't at the project to help the kids, they were there to help me. I have been a more passionate volunteer ever since.

Wendy Sheridan
Tampa, Florida

**My first volunteer experience** was sorting coats donated through a coat drive. It was better than I expected it to be. I remember feeling an overwhelming sense of peace, the feeling that I was making a difference not just in the lives of others but in mine as well, a feeling that got me so excited about volunteering my time at future projects.

Laurie Ritterbach
Pittsburgh, Pennsylvania

**I had some bad things happen** to me on a past birthday. Now I always make sure to volunteer on my birthday, and this act gives me the opportunity to feel better about myself and not let bad experiences control me. Volunteering is healing and a way to remember my blessings.

Denise Riebman
Boston, Massachusetts

**Volunteer projects bring fun into your life** and force you to slow down and smell the roses. Usually I end up doing things I'd otherwise never get around to. For instance, we often take the kids we mentor to an IMAX movie and then sit around and chat afterward. This is the kind of activity I would love to do with my friends if I ever made the time!

Laurie Finch
New York, New York

**Friends are made by serving them** or serving with them. Four people I served alongside at a nursing home became some of my closest friends. They were there for me when my mom ended up in a nursing home after her surgery went badly. When she died the day before finals, my friends from the nursing home were there to support me and take care of me, helping me get through finals, pack, and get home in time for the funeral. Life is fuller and more manageable when you spend a little time each week thinking about others instead of yourself. A life without service is no life at all.

Jessica Jones
Bowie, Maryland

**Through volunteering as a teacher,** I have overcome my fear of public speaking. You can't run a karate class without saying something to the kids!

Jessica Marshall
New Windsor, New York

## Voices of Change: Paul Terry

"What if hope is a lie?" It was intended as an impassive question by a brilliant physician researcher at Park Nicollet, a health system in Minnesota where I work. We were debating whether measuring resilience gave us insight into quality of life for people living with chronic health problems. Perhaps this prominent healer supposed, as Ben Franklin did, that "he that lives upon hope will die fasting." Could hope be a false promise, an impediment to action? The question came back to me for many days, and each time I thought of Beaulah Muchira, a talented, captivating, and passionate program manager of a Hands On Network affiliate located in Harare, Zimbabwe.

As cofounder of SHAPE Zimbabwe, an HIV prevention organization in Zimbabwe, I first encountered Beaulah as a student leader. She and other students composed songs with HIV-prevention lyrics that were played on radio stations throughout Zimbabwe.

People often ask if working on prevention in a country devastated by HIV/AIDS is depressing, and I've always responded that the young people, with their resilience and zeal for life, give me hope. Indeed, AIDS activists in southern Africa often reinterpret the HIV acronym to mean "Hope Is Vital."

Samuel Johnson wrote: "Hope is necessary in every condition. The miseries of poverty, sickness, and captivity would, without this comfort, be insupportable." Consider the projects that Beaulah is leading for Hands On Zimbabwe (HOZ), and consider whether hope, comfort, and action can coincide. The HOZ Winter Warmer project provides 39 child-headed households (133 kids), mostly AIDS orphans, with warm clothing, food, blankets, and school fees.

Barbara Kingsolver, an extraordinary novelist, wrote: "The very least you can do in your life is to figure out what you hope for. And the most you can do is live inside that hope. Not admire it from a distance but live right in it, under its roof." I've come to hope for many things, most often related to the health and welfare of those I've come to know and love and serve. Poverty and sickness will forever rain down. Yet, Beaulah's is a magnificent roof, and I've been proud to seek comfort under it.

I don't know if hope is a lie. But I believe those who live upon hope die sated and warm.

*Paul Terry, Ph.D., is President and CEO of the Park Nicollet Institute (www.parknicollett.com), an organization that engages in research, education and innovation to improve the quality of public and private health and healthcare. Paul taught public health in Zimbabwe as a Fulbright Scholar and has also been a Kellogg Leadership Fellow.*

The American Community Garden Association recognizes that community gardening improves the quality of life for people by providing a catalyst for neighborhood and community development, stimulating social interaction, encouraging self-reliance, beautifying neighborhoods, producing nutritious food, reducing family food budgets, conserving resources, and creating opportunities for recreation, exercise, therapy, and education. To learn more, visit www.community garden.org.

**Volunteering gives you confidence** and superhuman strength. When something just has to get done, you do it. I was on a gardening project with six or seven other women. Some equipment was brought in on the back of a pickup truck that somehow got stuck on some train tracks. So all of us grabbed the back of the truck and lifted it off the tracks! That felt amazing. I am now officially a superhero.

Beth Senko
New York, New York

**I began volunteering to feel more connected** with my hometown. I was playing professionally for a string quartet, and although I was based in San Francisco, I traveled a lot. I felt a little scattered and disconnected until I started volunteering at a transitional house, helping kids with their homework.

After that, it was great to be on the road, but I always knew I was coming home to my kids. Some people like volunteering because it offers you a chance to meet new people. I like to volunteer because it's a nice break *from* meeting new people all the time. When I'm working with my kids, there's no need to introduce myself because they already know me. It's a relief to get beyond the small talk.

Ann Gregg
Boston, Massachusetts

**The people you meet through volunteering** are like no one else! I once met a 104-year-old woman. She told us amazing stories, and when we had to go, she told us that she loved us. Days like that, you feel like you're seeing living history. It's sad that some people miss out on those experiences. When else would you meet someone like that?

Chris Carey
New York, New York

**Professionally, I work a desk job** and so I find the physical and tangible aspects of volunteering very satisfying. I bag groceries for AIDS patients and their families. It not only feels good to do actual, physical work, but I love the real results. The shelves are empty when I get there; the shelves are full of ready-to-go groceries when I leave.

Carol Rehder
Nashville, Tennessee

**A bonus of volunteering** is the quality of the people you will meet. I think there is something intrinsically special about people who volunteer. It's easy and natural to love your friends and family, but it takes a really extraordinary person to love a stranger. You really have to reach down deep to do that.

Bob Alden
San Diego, California

Visit www.senior corps.gov or www.civic ventures.org to find out how you can get involved, share your experience, and make a difference in the world.

## Professionally Speaking . . .

**Volunteering can teach** you new business skills. When I first started my work with the Make-A-Wish Foundation, I had no experience in accounting or marketing. But I had to dive right in and learn those skills quickly. Service made me a better person *and* a better businessman.

Pat Morris
Miami, Florida

**The managerial skills I've learned** through community service would have cost me thousands in tuition. Through my volunteering, I am routinely in different cities and countries and exposed to changing technology, language, and skills. I am a student of the world.

Sheri Frost
Crestview, Florida

**Volunteering looks fantastic on your résumé.** As soon as interviewers read that you've served at all, they really seem to warm up. Volunteering experience sets you apart from the competition and makes you seem special.

Amihan Makayan
San Francisco, California

**Volunteering is a great way** to find paying jobs. The volunteer work I did in college helped me land my first full-time job!

Devin Rucker
Atlanta, Georgia

**I am currently studying to be a social worker.** As a volunteer, my interactions with diverse groups of people has helped prepare me for my professional goals.

Krista Strobel
East Lansing, Michigan

**Volunteering is a great way to practice** other skills. I know a woman who wants to start her own catering company, so she volunteers at every cooking-related project she can find.

Cindy Huggett
Raleigh, North Carolina

**Volunteering is a great way to test-drive** a career. I always thought I wanted to be a teacher. Then I volunteered to teach. I realized it was not what I wanted to do!

Tamika Brown
Atlanta, Georgia

**I learn a lot about how to get** the most out of life from the people I serve. I once helped out at a free concert for seniors. Some of these people were blind and didn't have any hang-ups. The music was playing, and their joyfulness just happened with no self-consciousness. I was touched by how they were swaying, dancing, moving their heads, and smiling. I envied their ability to lose themselves in the music.

Carol Rehder
Nashville, Tennessee

Founded in 1924, the American Association of Zoological Parks and Aquariums, now known as the American Zoo and Aquarium Association (AZA), is a nonprofit organization dedicated to the advancement of zoos and aquariums in the areas of conservation, education, science, and recreation. Visit www.aza.org for more information.

**Service can make you feel needed** and important. At work, you may be the low person on the totem pole, and you may get all the uninteresting jobs, but when you give your time to a project, then you're the CEO of volunteering!

Laurie Finch
New York, New York

**My volunteer service with the zoo** is a stress reliever. I'm a financial adviser, so after a focused day at work, going to a meeting at the zoo and talking about where we should move the tapir or how we're going to fund the penguin exhibit is a relief. Those meetings are some of the most fun I will have all day.

Cam Ragen
Seattle, Washington

**As an only child,** I grew up always wishing I had siblings. Now that I volunteer with kids—many of whom I have kept in touch with over the years—I feel like I finally have little brothers and sisters.

Chris Carey
New York, New York

**Volunteering has given me a more** accurate picture of our society. I connect with segments of society that are hidden. Through volunteering, you can meet foster kids and the mentally ill, and if you do hospice work, you will meet the dying. Service has made me a lot more aware.

Rosaline Juan
San Jose, California

> "The way you get meaning into your life is to devote yourself to loving others, devote yourself to your community around you, and devote yourself to creating something that gives you purpose and meaning."
> Mitch Albom

**In high school,** I was required to complete 75 hours of community service to graduate, which I did. Then, when I was in college, my brother was diagnosed with Lou Gehrig's disease and my cousin with cancer, both within the same week.

Three years later, they died about three weeks apart. I was 21 and overwhelmed with grief. I thought back on my life, trying to remember what things had brought me joy and stability in the past. One of those things was service. So I joined AmeriCorps. The ability to effect change was so healing, and it also moved my focus away from my personal problems.

Emily Gilliland
Portland, Oregon

79

**Over the last 10 years,** volunteering has evolved into more than just a passion for me—it truly has become an addiction. Since emigrating from the Philippines to the United States upon my graduation from medical school nearly 45 years ago, I have been regularly involved in various civic and community activities over the course of my surgical career. But it was my first experience with a surgical mission to the Philippines in 1995 that made me realize my purpose in life was not only to go to the United States and "do good" relative to my career and family. I realized I now had the means, capacity, and ability to serve helpless, disadvantaged people in my home country who could not afford surgical care.

After that first mission trip with the Society of Philippine Surgeons in America (SPSA), I started raising funds and securing in-kind donations for future missions by writing letters to friends, colleagues, pharmaceutical companies, and other organizations. I also took the helm as a team leader of the surgical mission teams. Each year since then, I have organized and traveled with 30 to 40 other volunteers (20 of whom are surgeons of various specialties) on a mission trip to an island of the Philippines where our surgical services are urgently needed. In one week, our mission team performs approximately 300 surgeries, and we have conducted more than 3,878 surgeries since starting this amazing journey.

Helping so many people recover from pain and improve their lives has been truly transforming for me and other volunteers on the SPSA mission trips. We know we can't wipe out disease and infirmities, but we are committed to "putting a dent" in the misery and helplessness of the needy and poor. I hope to be blessed with many more years of service to my fellow Filipinos, continuing my life's true purpose on this earth.

Manuel A. Cacdac
Terre Haute, Indiana

## Editor's Note

Service offers a lifetime of possibilities—it allows people to develop friendships, cultivate values in their children, exercise new skills, develop their professional networks, and to give back in retirement. I have come to know some truly extraordinary seniors who have dedicated their retirement years to service. One of my favorites has been Miss Liller Tenant, who started out as an administrative volunteer at Hands On Atlanta and grew into our extraordinary organizational matriarch and receptionist. She continually thanked us for letting her volunteer. She joked that it saved her from spending all day at home with her husband!

## Lifelong Benefits

**Doing service can strengthen** your bond with your child. Rather than spending $15 to $20 at the movies, take your child to beautify a park with his own little bucket and shovel. Let him know how he has helped make a difference in that park, by picking up that trash or planting some flowers.

If your kids see a movie, they want to share it with their friends, not you. But if you put a day into service, learning together, you can continue that bond and that sharing at home. It's something you'll always have.

Genora Crooke
Atlanta, Georgia

**Your children will be more appreciative** if they volunteer. My daughters volunteer for Project Birthday, which throws birthday parties for the children in the homeless shelter. As we were pulling into our driveway after our first party, my daughter Katsumi said, "I'm so grateful for my house!" She no longer takes for granted all that she has.

Nina Schwarzwalder-Watanabe
Elk Grove, California

**Being involved in service** from a young age gives kids confidence they might not otherwise have. When I was in my early teens, I volunteered for the Mondale/Ferraro campaign. People ask me now if other kids made fun of me for being politically involved. Interestingly, I can't remember. I was so into the campaign. I was clueless; I didn't care! I felt so strongly about what I was doing that it never occurred to me whether it was "cool" or not to volunteer.

George Theoaris
Des Moines, Iowa

**It is so important to get outside** of your comfort zone when you are serving. To truly gain empathy about what is going on, you have to be completely immersed in that other world. You have to get involved and put yourself in situations that stretch you. People who just live their lives in insular ways and without that connection to others cannot gain a true understanding of what is going on. You can't force people to reach out. But without being in someone else's environment, you can't really understand the need that is there.

Diana Epstein
Berkeley, California

## Voices of Change: Ann Fudge

My commitment to community service really began in childhood. Growing up, my parents always helped families that needed assistance. They drew me into their efforts, whether we were collecting clothes or toys or funds, and we did them as a family. At school, we collected money for children around the world. And we always talked about why it was important and necessary to actively engage in your community, whether it was your neighborhood or some far-off place in the world. These early experiences left me with the understanding that everybody can make a difference. You don't have to do large things, you just have to do something. My husband and I have tutored kids. We've worked in soup kitchens. We've been Big Brothers and Big Sisters. There are so many ways to help. The important thing is to get out there and do it. Sometimes it's just one little thing you do that helps a person.

*Ann Fudge is the chair and CEO of Young & Rubicam Brands. She is the 2002 recipient of the Harvard Business School Bert King Award for Service to the Community, which honors achievements that purposefully benefit the community in the political and community development arenas, as well as personal commitment to being of service to others.*

**"Warning: Severe Flood Watch—Sacramento County"** flashed across our television screen. I looked outside, where our neighborhood street had turned into a river. I was 12, and my sister and I were very eager to blow up our raft and go out for an adventure, but my dad had warned us that if the levee broke, our house would go under. With the water nearing our garage door, my dad carried me out to his truck and off we went in search of sand.

My dad had one mission: to fill up our sand bags and get back to the house. But then we noticed some people who were unable to fill their own bags. We spent more than two hours shoveling sand for women and seniors: my first volunteer experience during a disaster. Little did I know how this would change my life and perception of the world over the next 13 years. Although it doesn't sound like much, it was the gateway to my career in AmeriCorps, where I would serve my country as an active citizen for the rest of my life.

Christine Bartlett
Phoenix, Arizona

**Volunteering has allowed me to do things** I would have paid money to do. I am a huge soccer fan, and I once was able to volunteer as an assistant press officer for World Cup USA. I acted as an interpreter, trained about 200 volunteers, and even escorted photographers onto the field. My childhood dream was to play in the World Cup, but this was close enough!

Andrew Leone
Fort Lauderdale, Florida

## Heart Strings

**For single people,** volunteering is a fantastic social bridge. I personally hate small talk, and working together on a project prevents having to engage in it. Service gives you something to do besides sitting around. If you are a shy or anxious person, meeting people this way is far superior to going to bars where you're in a dark room, shouting over loud music, and talking to someone who's probably not sober.

Sandra Hamel
Sacramento, California

**Serving others can help mend a broken heart.** Eight years ago, my long-term relationship broke up. When it finally ended, I stayed at home for two months and felt very sorry for myself. I realized I needed to snap out of it. Suddenly, a light went on: I should volunteer! I volunteered at a project that involved doing arts and crafts with abused and neglected kids. Helping these kids really put things in perspective for me: My problems suddenly seemed small in comparison to what they were going through.

Bob Alden
San Diego, California

**Volunteering won't expose** you just to new people, but really great ones! I've met some of my best friends through serving, and I even met my boyfriend this way. I believe that the people I meet while volunteering are the cream of the crop—more interesting, more involved, and nicer.

Heather Alexakis
Forest Hills, New York

**New York Cares was featured** in *Time Out New York* as the third-best place for singles to meet people. I would love to say that every single person who volunteers is altruistic, but the truth is it doesn't matter why you serve. If you're volunteering to meet people, that's fine!

Liath Sharon
Atlanta, Georgia

**Volunteer—it's like giving** the world a great, big hug.

Kerrin Grace
Boston, Massachusetts

## Voices of Change:
## Andreliz Bautista

"

I come from a long line of volunteers. Both of my grand-mothers and my mother devoted much of their lives to help-ing others, so you could say that volunteering is in my blood. From a very early age, I signed up for walkathons, helped in soup kitchens, and participated in food drives, but I surprised even myself when, in my senior year in college, I signed up for a two-year commitment to serve in the Peace Corps.

As a volunteer, I lived in Debere Gati, a small hamlet nestled in the rolling, arid hills next to the Say River in Niger. I clearly remember the day that Nelson and Peter (my Peace Corps trainers) introduced me to the village. One minute I was in an air-conditioned Toyota Land Cruiser enjoying the scenery of the African bush; the next I was dropped literally in the middle of nowhere, in 110-degree desert heat, with the only English speakers within 10 miles rapidly disappear-ing in a cloud of dust.

I stood there armed only with my duffel bag, my language and gardening notes from a three-month training session in Niamey (the capital of Niger), a year's supply of toilet paper, and with what seemed to be the entire village of 250 people staring at me. I'm certain they were thinking to themselves, 'They sent her to help us?'

At that moment, I wasn't really sure how I could help myself, let alone anyone else. I was briefly afraid that I would remain frozen in that position until my two years were up and another Land Cruiser returned to take me back to the airport. Thankfully, Delo, the brother of the village chief, soon greeted me with a warm smile and led me to the quarters the villagers had built for me. My new home was the newest mud hut in the village, with an outdoor bed, a latrine, and a beautiful dune fence made out of dried millet stalks. Villagers from all over Debere Gati came to welcome me with everything from blankets and baskets to goat's milk and a live chicken. Most of the villagers couldn't even afford shoes, and I was truly overwhelmed by their generosity.

It didn't take long for those strange faces to become good friends and a surrogate family. They treated me as one of their own and insisted on feeding me every night even though they barely had enough for themselves. Their problems became mine and vice versa: When the harmattan (a dry, dusty wind that blows through West Africa) caused my thatched roof to cave in, the village came together to fix it and provided me temporary shelter. When the millet needed harvesting before the locusts approached, I was in the field before dawn alongside every other villager to save what we could. Together with financial support from the African Food Systems Initiative Program, the people of Debere Gati and I were able to build cement wells, create community gardens, and bring in the Nigerian Governmental Service to help vaccinate infants and teach simple, homemade rehydration formulas to the mothers.

Nigerians are amazingly resilient, and they taught me the true meaning of 'Where there is a will, there is a way.' I am not sure how effective I was in helping my fellow villagers, but I am certain that I got far more from the experience than I gave. For that I will be always grateful to them. When I first arrived in Debere Gati, I felt sorry for my new friends because they seemed to have so little. Many years later, I believe they may be the happiest people I have ever met. I still miss the boisterous laughter I could hear from the neighboring huts while I read by lantern in my bed. They live hard lives, but they are confident that God will take care of them, and they are never more content than to be with their families and to be alive for another day. It's a wonderful way to approach life, and one we should all be so lucky to adopt.

*Andreliz Bautista is an entrepreneur who cofounded a highly successful restaurant group based in Washington, D.C. Her next venture, now in its startup phase, is an organic cosmetic business. She contributes to her local community through projects ranging from mentoring to chairing a fund-raising event for Girls Inc.*

## Voices of Change:
## Harris Bostic II

Oh, I remember the day so clearly when I signed the seemingly thousands of papers required to close on my first house. And, not just any house, but an old house with lots of charm, and in need of lots of TLC. I was terrified that I didn't know a hammer from a screwdriver.

'Just go and volunteer with Habitat,' a coworker at the Atlanta Committee for the Olympic Games (ACOG) told me, 'You'll learn everything you need to know about working on houses.' So for me, it started out very selfishly as 'Habitat for Harris.'

My first day at the site started at 7 a.m. with volunteers offering donuts, slapping on name tags, and giving an overview of what to expect. Around 4 p.m., I stretched my aching back and looked up at the wooden house frame that hadn't been there just hours earlier. 'Wow,' I said to another volunteer, 'I can't believe we actually made that!' Then one of the family members who would receive the house came over and stood back in awe too. That was the moment I understood Habitat's 'sweat equity': the truly hands-on investment family members put into building their own house.

That eye-opening Saturday begat another one, up to five more until the house was completed. When the family received their keys, my dirty shirtsleeve received several of my tears.

It was then that I realized I had become addicted to Habitat. I continued to volunteer every Saturday. Persuading ACOG to provide resources, I led the effort to build two Habitat houses. More than 200 volunteers participated in building the two homes, yet I wanted even more! So I convinced the two organizations to construct 100 homes in conjunction with the Centennial Olympic Games.

I not only learned the proper use of a hammer and screwdriver—plus drills, wrenches, saws, Sheetrock, and insulation—I learned that a little hard work, a lot of sweat, and a heart full of caring could take a selfish beginning on a journey that would end with many families' dreams of home ownership coming true.

*Harris Bostic II is currently a director with the American Red Cross Bay Area and formerly a Habitat Atlanta board member.*

ONE OF THE MOST REWARDING PARTS of my work at Hands On Network has been hearing stories of personal transformation from volunteers. Sometimes I hear the expected refrains, "I got so much more out of it than I was able to give" or, "I really discovered my community and my part in it for the first time by serving." Other times, I hear unexpected stories of consultants and lawyers who, without trying, expanded their client base through volunteering. I have learned from young people how they gained a new sense of confidence by leading adults in service. One volunteer who began tutoring on Saturday mornings fell in love with teaching and changed careers, going back to graduate school and eventually becoming one of the most distinguished principals in the public school system where she works. As you extend your hand, you will discover new people, skills, connections, and perspectives. In reaching out, you will find rewards and opportunity beyond what you imagine.

M.N.

# CHAPTER 4

# Climbing Mount Everest
## OVERCOMING OBSTACLES TO ENGAGEMENT

CHANGING THE WORLD IS HARD. If it were easy, it would have already been done. While our stories of change tell us of the bounty and unexpected gifts of service, they also tell us that we will run into obstacles and frustrations. As one of our change agents, Emily Garlock, tells us, "You have to prepare for being discouraged and have something ready to revive you."

There are small and large impediments to making a difference. A clear theme emanating from our stories is not to let the petty frustrations of your experience get in the way of your action or commitment. If you are working with an organization that is not using your time effectively, don't walk away. Give them feedback; jump in and help make it better. Don't let small impediments keep you from the transformational experience that service offers you. You can use obstacles to inform your perspective and see them instead as an invitation to get involved. Each wall can become a doorway.

It also helps to keep the big picture in mind—whether that's the person you are trying to help or the policy change you are trying to effect. At the same time that you are mindful of the larger issue, don't get lost in the immensity of a problem. You can lose sight of your own power to make a difference if you become overwhelmed by the magnitude of a challenge.

The principal guidance offered by our change agents is to sustain your commitment over the long haul, because burnout will come. Contributor John Gomperts tells us, "If you are out there working in your community and you aren't getting discouraged, you're not paying attention." Don't be swayed or bowed. "This is hard. Be strong," says one AmeriCorps member, speaking to a new group of volunteers. Don't be afraid to try different things, and be sure to nurture yourself in order to sustain your commitment. Refresh yourself with efforts that create short-term and tangible change, while always remaining mindful that systemic change comes over the long haul.

Most important, you will find strength and renewed energy in solidarity. "I keep it together," says Marlo Hyman, "by doing one thing: talking, talking, and talking." Find ways of sharing your experience; form a small support group, even of two or three people. You will find reinforcement and inspiration in sharing your service journey with others. Service can be a hard road, and the more help you get along the way, the greater your contribution will be, and the greater your personal transformation. The cathedral will get built, one block at a time, over generations. Find your place in the enterprise and be mindful of the larger vision.

**People mean well,** but sometimes they make excuses not to serve others. They say they feel so guilty working with people who have nothing. In truth, people don't want to admit that they're scared of other segments of society, of other cultures. But if you get over your fear, if you just put it aside for one day, you could be making a real difference in the world and wind up making yourself feel less guilty in the process.

Emily Horowitz
Miami, Florida

**When I feel burnt out,** I get out a box that I keep all my letters in. I read notes from friends and family thanking me for helping or listening. I remember that I have made a difference, albeit a small one, and it motivates me to keep volunteering.

Rebecca Frank
Westlake, Ohio

**When I was being trained** for a volunteer experience, the trainer told us to write a list of self-care things, hobbies we could lose ourselves in. I was skeptical that this was necessary, but I did it anyway. I wrote a list that included things like reading, taking baths, watching old movies, and hanging out with friends. I thought I'd never go back and look at it. Well, within the first two months, I was drained and couldn't think of how to pick myself back up. Then I remembered my list. Now, every night at 10:30, I read a book, and it totally helps. I even called that trainer and apologized for not believing her. She was right—you have to prepare for being discouraged and have something ready to revive you.

Emily Garlock
Pittsburgh, Pennsylvania

**I knew I wanted to join the Peace Corps,** but I had hesitations about resigning from my successful career, letting go of my cute apartment, and selling almost everything I owned in order to start a new, simple life in a third-world country. I found it very difficult to let go of my family and friends for two years, knowing their lives would all move on while my own would be in limbo.

Since 1960, when then-Senator John F. Kennedy challenged students at the University of Michigan to serve their country in the cause of peace by living and working in developing countries, more than 182,000 Peace Corps Volunteers have served in 138 countries all over the globe. For more information, visit www.peacecorps. gov.

But Peace Corps had accepted me, they had found me a position and country where they thought I would be well suited, and I had to give it a shot. In order to work through the hesitations I had and make the final decision to join, I allowed myself an "escape plan," giving myself permission to leave at any point during the service if I felt it wasn't working out. I never exercised this plan, but just knowing it was there helped me get through the two years (and three months of training).

Cynda Perun
Indianapolis, Indiana

**When I visit rest homes,** I worry about feeling awkward. When I'm on committees, I worry that I'll look stupid in front of other people—or I won't be able to do what they ask me to, and the event will be a flop. To overcome these feelings, I think of the quote that says, "It's all right to have butterflies—just get them to fly in formation." Push through it, and you'll always be glad you did. (None of my fears have come true yet.)

Rebecca Riding
Charlotte, North Carolina

**Sometimes it's true that if you're good** at something because you're passionate about it, you can end up promoted right out of your passion! I work in the administrative side of a nonprofit organization, and sometimes I start to feel detached from the purpose of my work. So to reengage and revitalize myself, I go back in and volunteer again. I go and "get shocked." I work with the hungry and the homeless, and it reminds me why I do what I do. I then go back and work even harder at my job.

Malikah Berry
Atlanta, Georgia

**Even after 10 years of volunteering** at the shelter, I have never gotten down. I think it's because I try not to think of the bigger problem, only my monthly service. I think, "This is where I get to make a difference. I'm going to contribute everything I can, right here." It sounds kind of cold, but not thinking too hard or too long about anything makes it easier for me to avoid getting discouraged.

Tripp Singer
New York, New York

**Don't stop working if things** at a volunteer event are not as organized as you'd like. You have to just go with the flow and make the best of it. Remember that the people who organized this are usually volunteers too! They may not be professional event or project managers. As long as everyone is safe, just work around any hiccups. If it's a matter of paperwork or the timing of something being off, be patient and remember why you're there.

Cindy Hugget
Raleigh, North Carolina

## The Starfish

A huge storm once swept through a seaside town during the night. In the morning thousands—if not millions—of starfish were washed up on the beach. Since they can't move on land very well, the poor starfish were left baking out in the sun until they died.

A man was walking along the beach that morning, and he thought about what a shame it was that all these poor starfish were suffering and soon to die. He even did what he could to try not to step on them. He soon came upon a young boy who was also walking carefully down the beach, but the boy was actually stopping and throwing as many starfish back into the ocean as he could. The man stopped the boy and said, "Son, there might be a million starfish out here. How can you possibly think you'll make a difference?" The boy looked at him, picked up another starfish, and threw it in the ocean. Then he said, "I sure made a difference to *that* starfish."

*adapted from* The Star Thrower *by Loren Eiseley*

**Never let one job or service opportunity** discourage you from your cause. Just switch up your roles and keep going! I used to be a social worker, but after a while it really got me down. I was always working with the adults who didn't want you there in the first place, and had to deal with all the paperwork and the legal system. I thought there must be a way to work with kids and not have to feel so frustrated and ineffective. So I switched: I became a camp director, and although that job has its bad days as well, I find it so much more rewarding.

Robin Longino
Greenville, South Carolina

**The best way to deal with burnout** is to acknowledge it. You have to know you're going to go through it. At AmeriCorps City Year, someone makes a very powerful speech, every year, to new corps members. The gist of it is, "You're dealing with the toughest problems and answering the toughest questions. This is not easy and not a cakewalk. It's going to be hard." It's almost a City Year motto: "This is hard. Be strong."

Sarah Trabucchi
New York, New York

> **City Year was founded in 1988 on the belief that young people in service could be a powerful resource for addressing our nation's most pressing issues. Visit www.city year.org for more information.**

**If things are not going well,** I know it is because I am supposed to learn something from the experience that I will need to know later. I just stay more alert so I can recognize and take advantage of the learning experience that is at hand. I view every second as a progression down a path to some destination.

Joe Mullin
Round Rock, Texas

**We all have our foibles;** we are all human. I volunteered one night at a shelter for homeless women serving meals. I placed a plate at a table for a woman who refused, saying she wasn't hungry. So I took the untouched plate to another table.

The woman I handed it to also refused it, saying she didn't want food that had been given to someone else. I politely explained that no one had touched the food, but she was adamant and demanded another plate. I was offended. Here I was volunteering my time, offering her a free meal that she had the gall to refuse. I felt that this woman should have been grateful for what she could get and that she wasn't in a position to be choosy. The rest of my evening was ruined, and I decided I wouldn't volunteer there again.

Thinking about the incident later, it occurred to me that I was really upset because my efforts had not been appreciated by that woman. But then I realized that I was doing volunteer work for selfish reasons, for praise and recognition. Just because a person is homeless doesn't mean that he or she has to settle for substandard service. Even though I felt she was being ungrateful and silly, it was her right to be, and it wasn't my place to judge her. We all deserve to be treated with respect and dignity, whether we own a home or live in a shelter.

Laurie Ritterbach
Pittsburgh, Pennsylvania


**You can't take responsibility for everything.** You can only do your part. So go ahead and plant that acorn today. Even if you don't ever see it grow up to be a big tree, you've done your part, and that has value.

Kim Smith
Portland, Oregon

**A couple of years ago,** I brought my infant son to the hospital with a broken leg. I'd had no idea how or when it got broken, so the hospital referred me to the Department of Family and Children's Services (DFCS), assuming that I had intentionally hurt my son or that the injury was in another way my fault. The state of Georgia ended up taking temporary custody of my son, and mandated that I take parenting classes in order to determine if full custody should be reinstated to me. Bewildered about the situation, but determined to keep my family together, I spent eight weeks taking classes at the Alpha Center.

Throughout the course of the classes, the instructor kept telling me that she thought I would be great for an AmeriCorps program starting in my city. So I took the opportunity to learn more, decided to join the Citizen Action AmeriCorps program a few weeks later, and started working with the East Point Community Action Team (EPCAT). During my first week at EPCAT (www.ep-cat.org), I received the results of my son's bone density test and learned that he had osteogenesis imperfecta, more commonly known as "brittle bone disease." After sharing these results with my case worker, and showing that I did not intentionally harm my son, the state returned him to my custody.

> "Only a man who knows what it is like to be defeated can reach down to the bottom of his soul and come up with the extra ounce of power it takes to win when the match is even."
> Muhammad Ali

Committing to service with AmeriCorps helped me to overcome this tremendous obstacle in my personal life. Being able to share my story has helped me to truly expand one of EPCAT's signature events, Stand for Children Day. This annual event is dedicated to the enrichment of children and parents through programs, activities, and service opportunities.

Sharon Underwood
Atlanta, Georgia

**I work at an animal shelter,** and unfortunately I see a lot of animals pass away. There was this really big, really beautiful, really sweet dog. She eventually died, and I remember crying my eyes out, but by then I was walking the next dog. For every dog that dies, there are a hundred sweet dogs that could still use your help. You can't always take time to mourn; you have to keep going.

Heather Alexakis
Forest Hills, New York

**I was hesitant to volunteer** with Habitat for Humanity. You see, I'm not the most talented individual when it comes to wielding a hammer. In fact, when our television station opted to report live from a Habitat site for the United Way Day of Caring, it was none other than yours truly who ended up whacking her finger with the hammer for all our viewers to see. You can't let things like that stop you.

Ronne Rock
Austin, Texas

" After the final no there comes a yes and on that yes, the future of the world depends. "
Wallace Stevens

**If you feel as if you have to** "overcome" something, then it may not be the right volunteer opportunity for you. Keep looking.

Penny Townsend-Quill
Rochester, New York

## Editor's Note

Two of the bravest volunteers I ever met were twin sisters in their early 20s who had severe cases of Tourette's syndrome. Tourette's is a heartbreaking disease that manifests itself in uncontrollable shouting (often of profanities), stomping, and other inadvertent physical motions. These sisters were victims of a cruel fate that isolated them, rendered them unable to work in almost any setting, and made them unwelcome even to their neighbors, who were offended by their noises and gestures. Out of this loneliness and frustration, they reached out and began to volunteer administratively in the Hands On Atlanta office. It was a difficult challenge. Shy and accommodating in spirit, the twins, against their will, would stomp and shout profanities throughout the office as we all struggled to find the humor and compassion to make the circumstances work. They volunteered with us for a number of years, giving all of us a new perspective and a huge respect for the enormous fortitude it takes for some people just to get through a day. The young women also found solace—they discovered companionship, a sense of accomplishment, and profound relief to be a part of the ordinary world of work and contribution. When I think of the obstacles that they overcame every day in order to act, it gives me great hope about what is possible.

**When my energy is low,** I keep myself motivated by using a little guilt on myself. If I'm tired on a Saturday morning and feel like sleeping in, I think of the child I will disappoint—the one who's counting on me to come and help him with his reading. If I sleep in, I'll be letting down a child. I just can't do that, so I get up.

Melissa Bieri
New York, New York

**Count up every little thing.** It recharges you to keep going. I remember once thinking I wasn't doing very much, and that those few hours out of my Saturday couldn't have meant anything significant to anyone. Then, after I had continued volunteering for a few months, I added up all the meals I had served and all the kids I had played with and all the rooms I had painted. I realized I had made a visible difference, one hour at a time, and I had fun in the process!

Wendy Sheridan
Tampa, Florida

**I keep my enthusiasm and energy** high by mixing up my volunteer activities. The sheer variety of volunteer opportunities out there is enough to keep anyone engaged. For example, I rotate between working with AIDS patients, to seniors, to homeless people, to Special Olympics, and then I tutor kids at shelters.

Amihan Makayan
San Francisco, California

**I look at keeping discouragement** at bay the same way a long-distance runner would. If you're trying to climb a big hill, it's not going to help you to stare at the top of the hill. Better to look down and focus on your feet and the next steps you will take. Focus on the road directly in front of you.

Max Stier
Washington, D.C.

**You can't give up, no matter what.** In 1991, during a big Jimmy Carter Habitat event in Miami, I was hit by a stray bullet from a drive-by shooting. It grazed my scalp and knocked my hat off. Right then, I realized that serving underprivileged areas could be very dangerous. And it was also then I realized that I couldn't let anything stop me from serving, not even a bullet. Boy, was everyone surprised when I returned to the job site the next day, head bandage and all. Some people who had intended to leave after the shooting decided to stay. Sometimes just showing up can make a statement.

Pat Morris
Miami, Florida

**Taking a bit of time off can really refocus you.** I coach girls' soccer, and toward the end of each soccer season, I am so exhausted. Hundreds of practices, games, phone trees, and parties; I just can't wait for it to be over. I think about how nice it will be to have so much time to myself. I often wonder if I should take a couple of years off, but then after a few months without it, I can't wait to get back onto the soccer field with my girls.

Trinette Marquis
Sacramento, California

**Don't get frustrated** if your first service experience is not an overwhelming, tears-in-your-eyes event. Your work is still important. If you keep going back, you *will* have that kind of experience. I've been doing community service for years, and a recent experience was one of the most touching I've had. I helped build a ramp for a disabled senior citizen, and I will never forget his face. When we completed the ramp, he said nothing, but he had a big smile. For the first time in a long time, he could walk out his back door onto his lawn with his walker. Talk about impact; talk about tears in your eyes!

Cindy Hugget
Raleigh, North Carolina

**Never lose sight of the influence** you are having. At a shelter where I tutored, one of the other tutors was working with a really young kid who kept talking about "when I go to college." We were amazed that this child, who barely knew where his next meal or bed was coming from, was be so certain that he would one day go to college. That impressed me and reminded me that we really were making a difference. We were helping these kids believe that they could become whatever they wanted!

Amihan Makayan
San Francisco, California

"Not everything that is faced can be changed, but nothing can be changed until it is faced."
James Baldwin

**There's a saying in Judaism:** "If you have saved one person's life, it's like you saved the world." Whenever I get discouraged, or feel like what I'm doing doesn't matter, I try to keep that saying in mind.

Lisa Tabak
San Francisco, California

**I keep myself motivated in service** by breaking down enormous tasks into small, workable parts. When I was working at Suited for Change, which pairs donated suits with people who need them for a job interview, I would stare at the huge pile of suits and think, "I'm never going to be able to sort through all of this!" But then I would tell myself that even if I got one-eighth of the way through it, at least a few people would get the right clothes for their interview today. That kept me going.

Tamika Brown
Atlanta, Georgia

**You just have to work to the best of your ability.** Whenever I get sad about the people I'm helping, I think of volunteering as firefighting. The firefighters can see a fire and either think about what it's doing to the people's house and their belongings, and how sad and horrible it is, or they can jump in and fight the fire. That's all you can do—and that's a lot! Jump in.

Chris Carey
New York, New York

---

**Suited for Change is a Washington, D.C.-based private nonprofit organization that provides professional clothing and ongoing career education to low-income women who have completed job training and/or job readiness programs and are seeking employment. For more information, or to donate, log on to www.suitedfor change.org.**

## Voices of Change: Ann Cramer

I am a child of faith; it was always a part of who I was. Consequently, I had always been involved in community service projects when I was growing up. My mother and father would walk for the March of Dimes, for instance, and it was those kinds of things that became an integral part of me as I walked through my life. I'm not someone who all of a sudden became a Christian or woke up one day and wanted to help; I just moved into the world as the person I am.

I think a lot of people are touched by the desire to serve. When I first came to Atlanta, I had compartmentalized my life. I worked at IBM, and then I had Junior League and church life and social reclamation work, but that wasn't how I wanted to live. So I just made it happen. I just kept walking in the right direction.

Now, my work with IBM allows me to be involved in the lives of children and youth, and improving conditions for families with IBM's investment in local communities. I feel lucky. I happen to work for a company that has the same values that I do. I'm married to a man who has the same values. I have a community that focuses on those kinds of choices.

The truth is, I'm always second-guessing myself. I can think of the million things I'm not doing, or not doing right. I think we all do that. I've allowed this self-doubt to become the catalyst for my continuing improvement process. I believe in reviewing, revising, and acting. Reviewing, revising, and *being*.

My husband and I say that you become old when you stop thinking and dreaming and being innovative. The city of Atlanta uses this slogan: Every day is an opening day. I see it that way, too. Every day is exciting. It's the idea of being awake to change, opportunities, and people. Being awake and being aware and staying active—that's really important. It is being part of the community. It is the village that helps all of us.

**Ann Cramer is IBM's director for corporate community relations and public affairs. She has served many nonprofit groups, including Georgia Partnership for Excellence in Education, United Way, Carter Center Board of Councilors, Woodruff Arts Center, and the Georgia chapter of the International Women's Forum.**

**One way I keep my energy up** is by surrounding myself with a good network of support. I'm not just talking friends and family—having people around who can really relate to your work is important. If such a network doesn't exist, start one! It can be small, just two or three people who understand each other's day-to-day struggles and accomplishments.

George Theoaris
Des Moines, Iowa

**If you are out there working** in your community and you *aren't* getting discouraged, you're not paying attention. That's why it is so important to work on a team. Stay around people who can buck you up and keep you on track, people who can share their methods of getting over frustration and discouragement. It's fundamentally frustrating work, community service, and you need a good support system to get you through the tough times.

John Gomperts
Washington, D.C.

**There is so much suffering** in the world right now. It would be entirely too easy to become overwhelmed by any number of things happening at this moment. The most significant thing that has helped me to cope has been making a commitment to a spiritual practice. Spending time every day with my breath and my body—through the practices of meditation and yoga—has kept me alive in the work that I do and allows me to keep putting one foot in front of the other. It's practice that deepens our awareness, our compassion, and our wisdom.

Claudia Horwitz
Durham, North Carolina

**If you want to quit,** just remember that time in your life (and we all have had at least one) when you really needed help. Grasp that feeling and remember how thankful you were that someone helped you, and how awful it may have been if they had not.

Stefani Hisler
Tampa, Florida

**When I hit a burnout phase,** I take a month or two off from volunteering to step back and realize that I don't have to do everything. I am only one person and can only do so much. Now I know that doing two or three volunteer things in a month is fine and just as appreciated.

Stephanie Hagyard
Belmont, Massachusetts

"Obstacles are those frightful things you see when you take your eyes off your goal."
Henry Ford

**If you're working on projects** where daily progress is less obvious, it can be helpful to mix in some other very tangible volunteer projects. On some projects, the progress you make every day is very evident, and this can be helpful.

Fred Northrup Jr.
Seattle, Washington

**Having volunteered with animal shelters,** rescue groups, and other community assistance organizations for about 15 years, I began working with Southern Hope Humane Society in Atlanta when it took over management of the county's animal services operation.

The American Society for the Prevention of Cruelty to Animals is 140 years old and helps to increase the demand for adoptable dogs and cats and simultaneously reduce unwanted litters. For more information, visit www.aspca.org.

My weekend work there usually involves shuttling shelter animals to vets and to off-site adoption locations, sometimes far from home. On my first out-of-town transport in 2005, we drove 47 dogs of various ages and sizes, including a couple of mother dogs and their pups, to a shelter in Connecticut a 1,000 miles away. I was eager to get the dogs to new homes in New England but apprehensive about the nonstop overnight journey. We arrived about 18 hours later with only a few barks along the way.

I felt a sense of relief and satisfaction once the dogs were safely delivered. I will be taking another 100 dogs along the same route to several shelters in New England; after Hurricane Katrina, I worked on transports and in devastated neighborhoods of New Orleans in search-and-rescue efforts for animals that were left behind. I would like to see more people offer some of their time, energy, and financial support to those who can't help themselves, both human and nonhuman. There's nothing more important or rewarding.

Bob Weiss
Atlanta, Georgia

**I want to tell the story of Ju-Hui Yang,** who moved from Taiwan to America and got married. This would have been a fairy-tale "happily ever after" marriage had her husband not died of cancer 16 months into the marriage. Having no job, a pending immigration case, and deep in mourning, Ju-Hui turned to volunteerism. Through her work with Triangle Impact, Ju-Hui made new friends, gained fulfillment from helping others, and saw firsthand that there is joy in being alive and making a difference in even the smallest way. I am glad to know that volunteering was able to help her through her pain and will forever be a part of her life.

Jeff Ware
Chapel Hill, North Carolina

**Pets 911 provides a free public service to ensure an environment where all animals are valued companions and have lifetime, loving homes. This network is a collaborative effort of all the animal rescue organizations and services across the country. To learn more, visit www.pets911.com.**

**Teaching kids anything is challenging.** I don't think I ever get through coaching a baseball practice without asking myself why I'm putting myself through this. The kids get frustrated, and that makes me frustrated. But anything that's worthwhile is going to be difficult. If it was easy, everybody would do it. So I dig down further and find a different way to explain who covers second base on a throw from the outfield.

Rorry Hollenbeck
Jamestown, New York

**Recently, an expectant mother** who attends my church went into labor at 27 weeks. She gave birth to a baby boy who weighed just over two pounds. Twelve hours later, her baby died. His lungs were not developed enough to sustain life. The grief that this couple experienced was unimaginable. I shared in their grief because they were personal friends of mine as well as members of my congregation. As I prepared to offer pastoral care, all I could think about was how difficult it would be for me to be present for them when I was so affected by their loss. But we stood in solidarity together, and I was able to be present with them while in my own place of suffering. I was there to be God's hands and God's heart for them. Oftentimes, people experiencing hardship just need you to be there for them and with them, of one accord and in unity.

Rev. Amanda Hendler-Voss
Atlanta, Georgia

**When I was serving in AmeriCorps,** I tutored kids living in poverty. That was probably one of the most difficult service projects I did, not so much because the work was hard, but because I felt as though I was only scratching the surface. We only worked with the kids for a couple of months, and in that time we were able to get a glimpse of what their lives were really like and what they really needed. You see the things that are going on in their everyday lives, and you realize that you can't be there in all the ways that they need. Their problems run so much deeper than just being behind in school. You are with them for a couple of hours each day, and then they have to go back to their world of struggle. At times it can be very discouraging. You just have to continue to do all that you can.

Diana Epstein
Berkeley, California

**Making a difference and trying to change** the world is not an easy feat. You must accept that there will be failures as well as successes. During my Peace Corps service, I was assigned to work with the local mayor and other government groups. One of my projects was to work with the tourism committee to boost tourism. I was very excited because our town had so much potential, and I had so many ideas of what we could do.

Unfortunately, the committee never wanted to meet, was constantly changing members, didn't follow through with tasks, and never used the resources or advice I had. I eventually had to let that project go and focus on other areas where my help was needed, like helping a group of students learn basic computer skills and holding an informal art class in my house.

Cynda Perun
Indianapolis, Indiana

---

Transitional housing programs assist homeless people who are ready to move beyond emergency shelter into a more independent living situation. Transitional programs allow individuals and families to further develop the stability, confidence, and coping skills needed to sustain permanent housing. To learn more about federal agency investments and results in assisting homeless families and individuals, visit the Interagency Council on Homelessness at www.ich.gov.

## Voices of Change: Kristen Roy

What began as a response to a sense of social obligation became transformed into a passion that drives my personal and professional life. I had read stories of homeless people in New York, malnourished children in third-world countries, and patients suffering from terminal diseases. I was sympathetic to their situations, but it wasn't until I was personally touched by each scenario that I became empathetic.

While a student at Marist College in New York, I immersed myself in textbooks on social justice issues. This education and awareness became the foundation of my volunteer interests and ultimately my career. Recognizing that, as a young student, I didn't have my own resources to address local hunger issues, I began considering creative alternatives. After a bit of research and with the support of college administrators, I established a meal distribution program that collected unused food portions from the campus cafeteria and delivered them to a homeless shelter in New York. Now in its fourth year, the program grew from delivering food twice a week to four times a week, with a rotating network of student volunteers. It astonished me that what began as a small idea could grow to a program generating substantial interest while addressing local hunger issues in my community. It certainly communicated that one vision can, in fact, create a chain reaction of commitment to others. Having spent time with the people receiving the donations, I quickly began to understand that we shared more similarities than differences. They no longer were statistics in my textbooks. Instead, they were people with real stories, personalities, and talents to share. I met the people of that shelter as "homeless residents," and left them as friends.

Then I moved to Tobati, Paraguay, an impoverished village in South America, for one year. Collaborating with a small nonprofit organization, Team Tobati in Connecticut, I taught English to poor children, volunteered in local hospitals, and worked on various social programs. I was able to establish a nutrition program for rural students that provided daily milk portions to malnourished children who would otherwise go hungry. My time in Paraguay was truly the catalyst of change for my own perspectives and led to a comprehensive questioning of values. No longer were hungry children and impoverished villages just images on my television screen. They became my students and my friends. During my last days in Paraguay, the Kristen Roy Educational Fund was established, which provides children with the resources to attend school.

Back in the United States, my boyfriend, Tory, who had been diagnosed with acute lymphocytic leukemia, was told he needed to undergo a bone marrow transplant. Although a successful match had been found, Tory underwent his preliminary treatments and became quite ill as the result of transplant complications. I stayed with him each day and supported his recovery, one that I was certain would come. But in December 2005, Tory passed away, and although I lost my boyfriend, I gained a new purpose, coupled with the strength and will that I learned from him and all the other patients I met in the leukemia wing of the hospital. In a last promise to Tory, I assured him I would fulfill all the plans that he and I had made, including the plan to help others in similar situations.

I have learned that true fulfillment comes from identifying and meeting the needs of others. When we share our natural talents and abilities for the betterment of others, we in fact find the best of ourselves.

*While a sophomore at Marist College, Kristen Roy established Project Marist Meals, a community outreach initiative aimed at responding to hunger needs at local shelters. Kristen later moved to Tobati, Paraguay, for 10 months to work on various development projects and to teach English to impoverished children.*

## Voices of Change:
## George Gervin

I was raised by my mother, who was a single parent. She raised six of us in the city of Detroit, and she kept us out of trouble by putting us in programs. Instead of running around on the streets, I was in the Boys Club or YMCA swim classes and basketball. I'm a product of these programs, and I know they work. When I was a youngster, they gave me something to do that kept me off the streets.

When I retired, it was looking back on this experience that made me want to do something for my community. My sisters and my mother and I live in San Antonio now. I decided that I wanted to develop a program that would help young people, so we started the George Gervin Youth Center, with programs that focus on disadvantaged kids and foster kids. From that, we started our charter school, the George Gervin Academy, which is for second-chance kids. It's a high school with core courses for grades nine to twelve, so our kids can study, graduate, and get a diploma. We've had that for nine years. We graduated 72 kids this past summer, and this year we have around 430 kids in the school. Over the years, we have touched the lives of more than 9,000 kids.

It's very gratifying. Some of the kids who have graduated come back and say, "Mr. Gervin, I'm so proud I went to your school. If I hadn't gone to your school, I might not have graduated. You know how important education is." Hearing that makes you feel like you touched somebody's life. When I go to graduation ceremonies and meet the parents, they tell me they are proud that their child finally turned that tassel to the other side and finished. You can't beat that compliment.

But I couldn't do this without the staff, the teachers, and the principal. It's a team effort. It's like basketball: I was a Hall-of-Famer and had a lot of success in basketball, but I couldn't have done it without my teammates. When you are working with a team, and that team works together like a fine machine, there is nothing better. That's what life is all about.

A child is raised by a village. It's important for people who have done well in life to think about someone other than themselves. Your success comes from others. We all need a helping hand. The reward you get by helping someone else may not be material. It will be emotional, and the gratitude that you get from lending a hand to someone else is unbelievable.

Go out and volunteer. Go out and help the homeless. Go to a food bank and pass out food and see the people you have touched. During Hurricane Katrina, I went to shelters and passed out food, just to see the people who had just lost everything. To be able to smile with them and give them a hug was something I'll never forget. Knowing that someone else cares for them might have given them the motivation they needed to get their life back. The worst thing in the world is thinking that no one cares.

*Only Wilt Chamberlain and Michael Jordan have won more league scoring championships than George "Iceman" Gervin's four, and he was the first guard ever to win three titles in a row. His career scoring average of 26.2 points per game is among the game's best, as is his combined NBA/ABA total of 26,595 points. In 1996, he was named one of 50 Greatest Players in NBA History.*

# REFLECTIONS

WE HAVE CELEBRATED INSPIRING, hopeful, and unexpected returns of service, but it is important to note that in trying to repair the world, we face the reality of suffering, overwhelming need, and bitter walls. There will be inevitable disappointment and despair. A friend of mine has been volunteering in a low-income neighborhood for almost 15 years. He has seen new initiatives for helping the neighborhood come and go: playgrounds built and then left to fall into disrepair, corporate and federal partnerships announced and then abandoned over time. He has coached a baseball team of young boys from this neighborhood and watched them grow into men. Many of them have met violent deaths or ended up in prison. How do we reconcile ourselves to our individual and collective failures to effectively meet the needs of our neighbors? What do we learn and how do we sustain hope? My friend has grappled with issues of race, privilege, and societal ills, and he has wrestled with them as personal and community demons. He keeps trying and he perseveres, against the odds and against the evidence. Perhaps our greatest victory is in sustaining the struggle and asking others to join us in solidarity of action and reflection.

M.N.

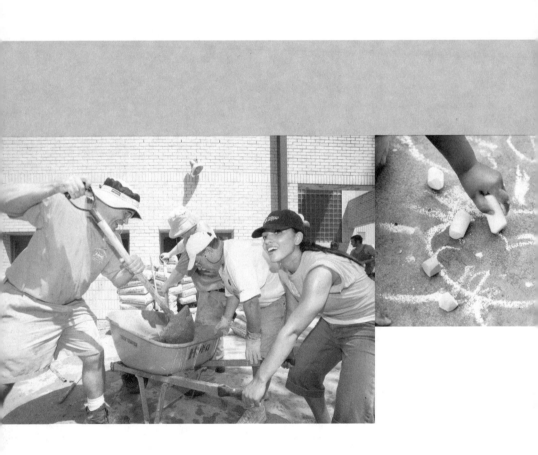

# CHAPTER 5

# It takes a village

## INVOLVING FRIENDS, FAMILY, AND OTHERS

HOW DO MOVEMENTS COME INTO BEING? Change starts with an individual, with one person believing that something can and must be changed. But change only becomes an enduring reality when individuals join together to act. Social change movements are often led by powerful individual change agents, but if you look closer, you will find that these individuals acted in concert with friends, family, mentors, and organizations. In working together, change is possible.

We need other people in order to sustain our own work in changing the world. We need the support, the fresh perspectives, and the solidarity. We also need the power of many in order to achieve lasting change.

How do we enlist others in our efforts to make a change? The most fundamental and important step is to ask. We know from our stories, and we know from research, that the most common reason people choose to help is simply that they were asked. The stories in this chapter tell us a lot about different approaches for asking—from showing people pictures to offering culinary incentives to appealing to their self-interest or pride in their community.

Remember that you are giving people a truly meaningful opportunity. You are doing them a favor by giving them an invitation to serve, to do something important and to change their world. You are inviting them into the transformational adventure of service. Don't hesitate to ask.

The stories in this chapter also remind us to make the experience fun and dynamic and to offer reinforcement and appreciation. This will keep others coming back to help (and will help keep us going as well).

Other advice includes calling upon people's sense of idealism, inspiring them without sugarcoating the experience. It is important to prepare people for what they are going to face. Also, don't forget to call upon people's talents; help them find the connection between their skills and passions and the needs of the world.

Perhaps most important, by incorporating service into your life, you will be a walking advertisement for engagement. You will inspire people without even knowing it; by being the change yourself, you will indeed create a ripple of change beyond your own imagining. You will also make one of the most important discoveries of acting—that you are not alone in your desire for change. When we engage in service, we not only change ourselves, we offer others the opportunity to change.

**People often skip important steps** when recruiting other volunteers. First, you need to build a relationship. You can build rapport even with strangers, and get them interested in serving. Simple things, such as making eye contact and finding commonalities. Use the same skills you use to make friends.

Second, you can't ask people for a hand until you show them your heart. Make sure you're passionate about the project, and make sure people know it. They'll be far more likely to join up with you.

Diamond Leshane
Atlanta, Georgia

**Phrase your recruiting efforts carefully.** I no longer ask people to write letters to their congressperson. I ask them, "Would you please be an advocate for the homeless?" Once they say yes, I then tell them how they can give a voice to these people.

Sara Needleman Carlton
Seattle, Washington

**Take every opportunity to inspire the people** you're serving to go out and inspire others. We have a motto among my group of volunteers: "Give someone a fish and they eat for a day. Teach someone to fish and they eat for a lifetime. But teach someone to *teach* how to fish, and an entire village eats for a lifetime." Whenever I help get others on the right track, I always encourage them to share their new life skills with their friends and family. Systemic change can happen on a grassroots level too.

Emily Horowitz
Miami, Florida

**New blood is crucial.** To keep an ongoing volunteer opportunity alive, there needs to be some new blood always going in. You can't let things get stale.

Chris Harris
Raleigh, North Carolina

**When I want to recruit someone** to come out to an event with me, I don't give them a chance to say no. I say, "What are you going to do tomorrow?" and wait until they say, "Nothing." I then say, "Great, you're coming with me to XYZ." Works every time, and they usually end up thanking me.

Jessica Shevitz
New York, New York

**When you're recruiting people for a job,** make sure you're appealing to their particular skills. For instance, many men offered to help when we asked them to build games for a fair. Regular guys, dads, feel more comfortable building stuff in their garages than they might coming into a school and volunteering there. Another example was our international New Year celebration. Our community has a large Laotian population that doesn't speak English well and feels they cannot participate in ordinary activities. We asked them to contribute by cooking their native Hmong egg rolls for the celebration. And they did! We managed to engage all parts of the community by asking them to donate their particular skills.

George Theorais
Des Moines, Iowa

**It is hard, but embrace the one volunteer you get,** then build from there. One person can make a difference in the environment, in another person's life, or for your project. Have a detailed list of work for the volunteer to do, train him appropriately, and be there for him.

Dawn Balzarano
Sacramento, California

**Remember that you can't create someone** else's experience for them—all you can do is provide them with the opportunity and let the experience take over from there.

Jeannie McNab
Seattle, Washington

"Train up a child in the way he should go, and he will not depart from it."
Proverbs 22:6

**How do I get my friends and family** to come out and volunteer with me? I bake! There's always food at my meetings.

Sherry Lynn Fazio
New York, New York

**Strike while the iron's hot.** If you're talking to someone about your volunteering, and they say, "That sounds like fun," tell them right there and then, "OK, you're signed up. See you next weekend."

Sara Needleman Carlton
Seattle, Washington

**Keep the joy alive in a project.** We were helping a missionary organization ship some things out. We had to help sack hundreds and thousands of pieces of clothing to ship to Africa. I turned it into a game to keep the youth and adults from looking at it as a job. We would race to see how much we could sack in one to three minutes. We got more done, and we were still smiling afterward.

L'Tonya Elias
Kansas City, Missouri

**Get yourself networked in communities.** The Internet is an amazing resource for this. Use search engines to find communities organized around your personal interests where you can connect with others. Then, when the time comes for recruiting, people have a sense of who you are and want to help your cause, or they want to help just to be associated with the community you've created.

Amy Woidtke
Seattle, Washington

**Matching people to the right project** is key in successful recruiting. Once you can figure out what motivates someone, then you can find a project that will tap into that motivation. The connection and the magic of service will happen that much faster. And, people will stick with service longer.

Emily Gilliland
Portland, Oregon

**I tell the people I'm trying to recruit** to come to a project three times. Three is the magic number. After three times it takes or it doesn't. You can't twist their arm.

Hal Cato
Nashville, Tennessee

**I always keep in mind** my friends' talents and abilities. I have a friend who's a graphic designer, and I always thought that I'd be able to use him one day. And one day I did. I asked him, last minute, to help our volunteer group design a mural. He came through for us.

Melissa Bieri
New York, New York

**When you're attempting to recruit adults,** you have to make it meaningful to them. Appeal to their sense of pride. Instead of saying, "We need help to beautify the local school," say, "Don't your kids deserve to attend a beautiful school?" or "If our school is dirty and run-down, what does it say about our community?"

Danielle Boyd
Atlanta, Georgia

**Expect the people you recruit** to have different levels of commitment. Some do it just to feel better about themselves. That will only carry them so far. The ones who have that urge to make a mark on the world will last longer.

Ashley Johnson
Pittsburgh, Pennsylvania

## Voices of Change: Lynn Monachese

During last year's Corporate Month of Service, I participated in a blitz of 10 playground projects. Specifically, I served at Atlanta's Barbara McCoy Park, where we worked to beautify a community through landscaping and mulching. This little community was built in the early 1900s, and many of the current residents had lived there most of their lives. Prior to our restoration project, the area had experienced severe storms and flooding. When we arrived, we could see that many homes had been damaged by the water, yards were still scattered with debris, and one home still had a large oak planted firmly in the roof. A large drainage pipe had collapsed in the middle of the park, and the city was still working to repair it. To add to the chaos, Hurricane Katrina had hit just a week before, and the area residents were preparing to receive Katrina evacuees into their homes. It was a mess.

But over the course of two days, a different picture unfolded before my eyes. These people had a sense of community that I hadn't witnessed in a long time. In two days, I saw a neighborhood of four generations come together with a common purpose. The neighbors told me stories about how wonderful it used to be to live there. They told me about the dogwoods that had lined the streets, now dead or gone. They asked if we could plant more dogwood trees to keep the history going, and we did.

That first day, I felt like I was helping to bring back a way of life for a community that could have easily fallen by the wayside had there not been people to help get the job done. How long would it have taken and what would have happened if we had not been able to be there? This renovation was restoring a part of the residents' history and was breathing life into the area.

Because the mulch had not arrived on time, we went back the following weekend to finish the project. The community residents were happily surprised that we did what we said we would do. One senior exclaimed, "I can't believe you're here! It's so nice of you to help us get this done. We've talked about it, and it's nice to see it finally happening!" A married couple with two small children commented on how happy they were that they could bring their children to play in the park, and their grandmother could take a walk in the same area. We were building community with the community, and we became, for a short while, a part of them.

Even more inspiring, while we were helping the community to rebuild, they were already uniting to help the Katrina evacuees rebuild their lives. Even with their flooded basements and debris-strewn yards, they were extending a helping hand to others.

I have been inspired to continue my community service. In addition to the service opportunities The Home Depot provides, I am on a leadership team for a church outreach program that benefits family violence shelters. This program supports women and their children by providing food and clothing and refuge. It extends the amount of assistance so that more people can receive. It's important for me to be part of the solution and therefore be the change. You can't just write a check. A check can't hammer a nail. A check can't put a pair of pajamas on a baby. When you lose everything, you only have your hands and your heart and the people around you.

*Lynn Monachese has been with The Home Depot for 8 years as a Relocation Coordinator in the Human Resources department. Some of her volunteer activities include putting together care packages for soldiers in Vietnam and Iraq; an 11-year leader for Boy Scouts of America as well as a Team Depot Captain.*

**When I want to recruit people,** especially young people, I'm kind of an nontraditional volunteer spokesperson. I don't present it as, "We need you! Please come volunteer!" I go to colleges to talk about community service. The first thing I do is put up a slide and say, "Here's what your résumé would look like. Employers will see that you have leadership experience through volunteering, and they'll be more likely to hire you than the guy who doesn't have that experience." I appeal to *all* the rewards of volunteering, not just the warm and fuzzy ones.

Derek Darling
Rochester, New York

**Making it easy for people is more** than half the battle. I think one of the main reasons people don't volunteer is because they're not aware of the service opportunities in their community. I tend to be the one to offer the opportunity. I'll do the research and find out the details of where and when a weekend volunteer opportunity is. All they have to do is come with me.

Todd Liebergen
Nashville, Tennessee

**To access a network of thousands of volunteer opportunities near you, or to locate tools to help you track volunteers, log on to www.volunteermatch.org.**

# BE THE CHANGE!

**When you're trying to get friends** and family to come volunteer with you, don't give them a chance to say no. I tell my people: If you want to spend time with me, this is how I spend it. Come on along. What do I want to do for my birthday? I want you all to come volunteer at a school with me! It's a way to both hang out and do something good.

Malikah Berry
Atlanta, Georgia

> Many leading companies are sponsoring volunteering to improve their company and their reputation. Why? Because participating in the community builds teams, improves staff morale, and helps attract quality staff, all while enabling companies to show that they care about the communities in which they're working.

**If you want to involve more people,** don't be afraid to ask your boss if you can talk about your volunteering at work. The worst she can say is no, but she just might say yes! We put out an e-mail and held an orientation, right here at work, after hours. This made it that much easier for coworkers to attend. You could also host a "lunch-and-learn" seminar about your particular volunteer project, start a series on volunteering, or have your company newsletter do a feature on your project.

Heather Alexakis
Forest Hills, New York

## Leading the Charge for Change

**If you are going to start up** an organization of volunteers, do two things: First, don't seek publicity too soon. Make sure that the infrastructure is there to handle the influx of people before the publicity runs. Otherwise, you will have a lot of wasted volunteers. Second, make sure your board of directors spends a lot of time getting to know each other. The board will govern the organization, and the directors need to be comfortable with each other.

Hal Cato
Nashville, Tennessee

**Make sure people first understand your mission.** I served at a food bank in San Francisco. They started with a five-minute orientation, giving powerful stats about how many were going hungry in the city and how many the food bank was able to feed. And then they sent us in the back to pack potatoes and sort bologna. People were energized to do this otherwise-boring work, because they had those stats in their head while they were serving.

Gregory Baldwin
San Francisco, California

**Even the most passionate volunteer** has a finite amount of energy for an organization. Use that limitation to an organization's advantage. For example, if you have people who have occupied leadership roles for five or ten years, new people will think they can never achieve a leadership role themselves. That squelches their ambition and new ideas.

In the organization I work with, people are not allowed to volunteer on the board of directors for more than three to five years. Aside from letting new people with new energy eventually rise to these positions, this time limit gives leaders the feeling of stewardship. It keeps things fresh for the board members, since from day one, everyone knows they will eventually have to find their replacement.

Anonymous
Seattle, Washington

**It's good to give people faith in themselves,** but you should also let them know that you are there to help. For instance, I started a program to encourage children to volunteer. One teacher said she didn't know where to begin. I gave her some ideas and told her that if she needed my help, she could always call me. Two weeks later, she *did* call me—to say that she had set up her "Socks for Seniors" program, which involved her kids going around to nursing homes and delivering socks to the residents. She got it done without my help. Just knowing she had that support was all the support she needed!

Susannah Fotopoulos
Nashville, Tennessee

**Be very aware that time** is important to people these days: If you promise there will be only one meeting a month, be sure there is only one!

Mike Hoyt
Raleigh, North Carolina

**A lot of organizations make** the mistake of looking for one-time hits from people as opposed to developing an ongoing relationship. Take a step back and let the people soak up the nonprofit's goodness at their own pace.

Cam Ragen
Seattle, Washington

**The most precious thing people** have these days is their time. You need to make them know that the time they spend on your projects will really make a difference. For instance, it's hard to recruit office volunteers here at Hands On Atlanta. We need them to do things like making photocopies, entering data, and so forth. There's no glamour to it. But I once sat down with a potential office volunteer and explained to her the history of the volunteer summit she was helping us plan. I spent an hour letting her know how her efforts would impact our community. She became very enthusiastic to pitch in.

Liath Sharon
Atlanta, Georgia

**I look at my grandson as a little plant,** and I want him to grow up giving. The roots have to sprout when they're young. By the time that tree is full grown, they're already developed. Start your kids early; make it part of their everyday life.

Genora Crooke
Atlanta, Georgia

"A community is like a ship; everyone ought to be prepared to take the helm."

Henrik Ibsen

**My first volunteering experience** was with my mom, when I was just seven years old. She used to visit an elderly citizen, and for a little kid, it was pretty boring. I went along for the ride, and although I resisted it at the time, I think it worked on me subconsciously. I can't remember a lot about when I was seven, but I do remember going to visit that older woman. I think having that memory is one of the reasons I volunteer a lot now.

Anne Corry
New York, New York

**When you're attempting to recruit children,** be savvy. Go about it the same way professional marketers and advertisers do. You have to compete on that level! Establish "product loyalty" early. Get them helping out when they are very young so that by the time they're older, they will just naturally want to do it. They will be programmed the same way advertisers program them to want certain toys or cereals.

Danielle Boyd
Atlanta, Georgia

# BE THE CHANGE!

**The best way to recruit your friends** and family is to show people pictures of you in action: "Here's a picture of me putting shingles on a roof." It gets to them and makes it real. It's not just a model in a magazine; it's me in there, working to make the world better. They begin to see that they, too, could be making the world better.

Emily Horowitz
Miami, Florida

Stay connected to your volunteer network by signing up with LinkedIn at www.linkedin.com. Here you can build your network of friends and contacts with just a few clicks.

**When you lead a team of volunteers,** you have to be willing to get your hands dirty—sometimes very, very dirty. I work at a center that sorts and packs bulk amounts of donated food. Sometimes we get perishable stuff at odd times of the year: for instance, 30 crates of peaches, some of them rotten. So the volunteers and I play "Fear Factor"—the game is to go through and sort out all the rotten fruits and vegetables. You haven't lived until you've experienced 500 rotting scallions in New York City in August.

Beth Senko
New York, New York

## Voices of Change:
## Baron Davis

My grandparents played a huge role in who I am today. I grew up in South Central L.A. There was anything and everything going on in the neighborhood. Lots of gang stuff going on; drugs. If it was negative, it was there.

I was on my way to being placed in a foster home, but my grandparents stepped in. They said they would raise me. They gave me morals, values, great parenting, and a solid foundation. To keep me off the streets when I was very young, my grandfather built me a basketball court for Christmas. When he did that, all I could think about was playing basketball. I had my own court; I practiced every day. Sports are a great way to keep kids occupied. It takes up a lot of time. We played every day from 3 p.m. until the streetlights came on.

There were few resources for kids in my neighborhood, but the ones we did have were good opportunities. When I was a kid, I thought it was the coolest thing for basketball players like Benoit Benjamin and Gary Grant to come to our neighborhood and pass out things at Christmas. Because I saw people doing things like that, I told my granny, "When I make it, I'll buy you a house." I've always been a giving person because of the example set by people like my grandparents. They fed people when they were hungry, no matter who they were.

Once I made it to the pros, I knew that was what I wanted to do. When you're young and you have a lot of money, you start by giving it away. But then you start thinking about where the money is going and how it might best be served. So I learned from several people what a foundation was and how to set one up. Now I have the Baron Davis Foundation, which helps put on events for charity each year.

Along with the Baron Davis Foundation, I've started an organization called Grandparents as Second Parents, and my foundation works with LA's BEST (Better Educated Students for Tomorrow), which is an after-school program that helps at-risk kids.

We also hold camps for kids that teach them not only basketball skills, but also life lessons. More than 2,000 people have come through our camps. The best thing is that 10 of the guys who went through my camp are in the pros, and others are getting college scholarships. That's the joy; that's the benefit.

Another positive story is my aunt. She used to be on drugs and was homeless, but she cleaned herself up. Now she feeds the homeless. She doesn't have a foundation: She's just one lady who cooks and feeds people twice a month and gives them clothes. She visits skid row every other week, giving out shoes and feeding 50 to 100 people. Now I'm working with her to start her own foundation so she can do more.

I feel that we're in this world to help someone. My mission is to help as many people as I can, because people have helped me. The reason I made it is because people around me helped me and wanted me to succeed. That was the only reason. I want to do it to see people happy.

*Baron Davis, a former McDonald's All-American and Gatorade Player of the Year, is a point guard for the Golden State Warriors. In 2004, he founded the Baron Davis Foundation, which aims to improve the quality of life for underprivileged and at-risk youth and their families in the Oakland/San Francisco Bay Area, New Orleans, and Los Angeles communities.*

**Don't forget about your new recruits.** A lot of people, at the end of a project, just say "bye!" Keeping in touch is key to growing a project.

Beth Fenger
Atlanta, Georgia


**The best way to recruit is to offer people** something concrete. Don't offer vague possibilities: Get their availability and tell them concrete events they can join. Put it on a platter ready to go.

Andrew Leone
Fort Lauderdale, Florida


**Finding volunteers is a little like being in sales.** You have to be able to spit out a great two-minute inspiring story on a moment's notice. I launch into my speech whenever I can, taking the opportunity to get people involved and helping. Every time someone turns me down, I don't think, "I'll never get what I need." Rather, I think, "OK, I just haven't found the right person yet. Who else can help?" I'm a salesman for service.

Diamond Leshane
Atlanta, Georgia


**Cast a big net.** Ask for more people than you need. It's like any negotiation. Shoot high, and you'll end up with enough people to fill your needs.

Gregory Baldwin
San Francisco, California

**Don't sugarcoat the work,** and you'll recruit a strong group of volunteers. There's a direct correlation between hard, tough work and deep fulfillment. Don't be afraid to use your volunteers. Don't be afraid to say, "Today is going to be really hard work."

Sarah Trabucchi
New York, New York

**One way that I recruit volunteers** for a homeless shelter is by arranging panels at local schools and universities. The panelists are all men from the shelter who sit down with the students and share their experiences. This catches people and draws them in. They leave the panel thinking: "I want to see what they're talking about." "Those guys were interesting; I want to help out."

Melana Pavich
Atlanta, Georgia

"Teamwork is the ability to work together toward a common vision; the ability to direct individual accomplishments toward organizational objectives; it is the fuel that allows common people to attain uncommon results."
Andrew Carnegie

**It's very effective when organizations partner.** For example, a local hospice partners with the local humane society. The humane society volunteers give so much of themselves and have to see a lot of animals put down. The hospice volunteers will regularly come in and help the humane society people through the grieving process. These partnerships give groups of volunteers the strength to keep giving.

Carol Rehder
Nashville, Tennessee

# BE THE CHANGE!

**Be organized.** People love to come to something organized that unfolds well. Present yourself in a volunteer-friendly manner. Don't overwork volunteers. Make sure they have a good experience while they're there, and always work around their schedules.

Lemuel Hubbard
Atlanta, Georgia

**My dad became involved through** seeing my efforts. When I first began my nonprofit work, he thought I was working for free, and he didn't understand why I would want to do this with my life. I grew up in a middle-class, mostly white area, and there were no well-known volunteering outlets, so it would never occur to him to serve his community. He sees it now and helps out a lot! He watches yard sales for educational materials and books that I can use. He helped unload and deliver coats during a coat drive. Ultimately, he is proud of what I do and why I do it, though it was hard for him to understand at first.

Julie Stephenson
Chicago, Illinois

> Men love to volunteer. Log on to *Essence* magazine online at www.essence.com/essence/dorightmen, and see their 50 "Do Right Men" of 2006.

**Be passionate but realize your job** is to find others who are also passionate, not to convince people who aren't passionate that they should feel as you do.

Adam Tritt
Melbourne, Florida

## Voices of Change:
## Bill McDermott

I was born with 20/20 vision, but my parents taught me early on to see the world through other people's eyes.

We lived in the real world with real people who dealt with real-world pressures. My folks made sure I understood what it meant—what it felt like—to be a disadvantaged kid with no parents, a single mom struggling to feed a family, or a hard-pressed senior citizen without much of a safety net.

I learned about empathy as a young teenager, when I helped my dad coach an elementary school basketball team. The guys were pretty good players, and we won championships, but many of their families had fallen apart because of economic or emotional pressures. So they relished the on-court relationships and mentoring we provided. I think the athletic allegiances we fostered redefined what winning is all about.

When I was in high school, I bought my first business, a local delicatessen. I met all kinds of people working behind the counter. This was a big lesson in diversity. I offered free delivery to help shut-in seniors at home; I extended credit to blue-collar customers who were trying to make it from paycheck to paycheck; and I treated high school kids like adults. This experience taught me about connecting to—and understanding—the community.

Flash forward 20 years: I was running a division of Xerox in the late 1990s when I represented the company on President Clinton's nonpartisan Welfare-to-Work Initiative. I liked this project because we helped move former welfare recipients from poverty into the workplace. Helping others fulfill their God-given potential in America's opportunity culture meant the world to me.

At SAP Americas, we deliver technology innovation and improve business results for thousands of companies in North and South America, while simultaneously elevating the quality of life for thousands of citizens from Chile to Canada. Best-run businesses must have a hard edge in the marketplace and a soft touch in the community so that the world can become a best-run place.

As a technology leader, we stress civic engagement for our employees and high-technology learning for our communities. Last year, one-third of our nearly 8,000 employees volunteered to help the community; this year, we have a 40 percent engagement target.

I have been impressed by KIPP, the Knowledge Is Power Program. By eighth grade, 100 percent of KIPP students out-perform their school districts in math. These results have encouraged SAP Americas to financially support KIPP's work.

We live in one interconnected world. Each time our software solutions help a company, we add to the global economy. That helps create better lives for families. When you have an improving standard of living, there's hope. And hope is a pre-requisite to peace and prosperity.

Earlier this year, I was blessed to receive the Yitzhak Rabin Public Service Award. Rabin tried to create a better world. He once said: 'Man is not made of steel. He has a heart and soul. He cries and laughs. He loves and hurts … he is flesh and blood.'

For me, those are words to remember—and, hopefully, to live by—as I try to see the world through other people's eyes.

*Bill McDermott is the President and CEO of SAP Americas and a corporate officer of SAP AG. McDermott is an active community leader and advocate for social responsibility in business.*

# BE THE CHANGE!

**I was in Biloxi visiting** the Chamber of Commerce when a small group of volunteers and residents began talking about all of the work that was being done to rebuild the area after Hurricane Katrina. The volunteers were focused on the value of the labor—gutting houses, cleaning streets, helping to reopen schools—when one of the residents interjected. "Doing all of the grunt work is not the greatest thing that you volunteers have done here," she said. "After a disaster like this, you all have helped us to believe that there is still a future here. You've helped us to rebuild not only our homes, but our psyche, and envision what can be."

Margarette Purvis
Atlanta, Georgia

**If you catch someone doing something right,** don't just think it—say it! I often lead a group of volunteers, and we have planning meetings to organize our service. During the meetings we do introductions, and people tell a little about themselves and what they do. I always make sure I interject how much good each person is doing and in what way I appreciate their work.

Sandra Hamel
Sacramento, California

**If you want people to come out,** lose the guilt. Making people feel guilty doesn't work. What does work? Fun! We make our events as fun as possible. We also throw some networking stuff in. So then, instead of saying, "There are so many people who can't read and need your help," our group says, "Come to a fun thing. Come meet other people!"

Joel Kunkler
Rochester, New York

## Voices of Change:
## Ruth Messinger

"The single observation that has most influenced my life and my choices comes from Rabbi Abraham Joshua Heschel, who wrote: 'In a free society, where terrible wrongs exist, some are guilty, but all are responsible.' There are wrongs in our communities, in our country, and in the world, and we cannot allow these wrongs to pass unnoticed. Nor can we retreat to the convenience of being overwhelmed. We can always take actions to assume responsibility, address the problem, and make a difference in the world.

To become better able to do this work, it is important to get outside yourself, live someplace very different, immerse yourself in a culture that is not yours. Learn from where you are and those you are with, and get to know yourself and understand your own values in the process. My experience with this advice was not intentional, and in today's globe-trotting world it does not seem that dramatic, but it was for me at the time, and it changed my understanding of the world.

At age 22, I moved with my husband from New York City, where I had lived most of my life, to rural western Oklahoma. I found myself in a town of 11,000 people, none of whom shared my background or experience. Most of them had never met a Jew, and they were some mix of friendly, curious, and innately distrustful of everything I represented.

I quickly realized that when people in Oklahoma discussed the weather—also an endless topic of conversation in New York—they were not just talking to hear themselves: They were talking about crops and whether or not they would have the money to get through the year. I learned that almost every one of my classmates at the University School of Social Work were the first in their families to go to college, much less graduate school, and that two of them had lived through the fierce year of integration of Central High School in Little Rock as students from white opposition families.

When I started as a social worker a year later, I worked with families of widely diverse backgrounds in communities that discriminated fiercely against Native Americans and blacks, and with a local county governance structure that epitomized 'old boy' attitudes. The judge, attorney, and sheriff regularly told me that they had never before met a New Yorker, a Jew, a woman in a position of authority, or someone who talked so fast.

It was in learning to work with these officials, in finding the foster families I needed in tiny, local Bible-Belt fundamentalist churches, and in learning the worldviews of Native Americans, farmers, railroad workers, and long-distance truckers that I learned who I was and what I valued. I learned the most about understanding others, and undercutting stereotypes and prejudice.

That education stood me in good stead in the work I did for 20 years in local government and in the work that I do now as executive director of American Jewish World Service, an international development organization. It explains why we run an array of service programs at AJWS that place everyone from teenagers to skilled adult professionals with our projects in the developing world. Our volunteers share their expertise or lend their muscle to people trying to improve their communities. More important, they share themselves, so that villagers and volunteers both come to a new understanding of the other and a deeper understanding of themselves. They learn, as I did, what matters most to them, what their values are, and how to live and share those values with others. They come back saying the experience transformed their lives.

We learn the most from experience and from others—often those whom we least imagine to be our teachers. We learn from whatever we can do to get outside ourselves—to spend time in a different culture, to ask others who experience the world very differently, to deliberately choose to do things that are hard to do.

*Ruth W. Messinger is the executive director of American Jewish World Service, a humanitarian organization providing support to grassroots social change projects throughout the world. To learn more about this organization, visit www.ajws.org.*

**When I got my first job,** I was so excited that my employer, Accenture, had an active corporate volunteer program. Working for an employer that embraced service helped me wrap my arms around Atlanta and deepen my dedication to service.

For the company's annual volunteer events, especially Hands On Atlanta Day, we organize projects for hundreds of volunteers. Organizing activities for such large groups requires a lot of coordination, and our planning teams start months in advance. We create detailed to-do lists for every task. We secure tools from the Atlanta Community ToolBank, and we purchase and transport supplies from Home Depot. I've learned it's tough to drive a 24-foot truck down the curvy streets of Atlanta, but somebody has to do it.

We've repaired schools. We've built nature trails. We've painted people's homes. We've installed computers and network equipment. In exchange for our efforts, the community has shown us so much love. One time, a group of students from KIPP WAYS (West Atlanta Young Scholars) Academy, a local charter school, came to show their appreciation for our service by singing us songs. We were so happy when they stayed to help paint some murals that would inspire them to continue their education. One woman on the YMCA staff cried when she saw how we rewarded her daily efforts by turning a dull, boring cinder-block room into a peaceful oasis. I even had the son of one volunteer tell me as his little hands were helping to plant flowers, "I love volunteering."

Aside from the obvious benefits to the Atlanta community, I believe we have a better Accenture community because of our service. Volunteering gives newer employees opportunities to plan and lead projects in a safe environment. It also gives us a chance to bond together, meeting people we might never meet during the course of our workdays. If it weren't for volunteering, I might have never met my husband!

Lynn Coddington Gilbert
Atlanta, Georgia

**The first volunteer project** that my son David (now 7½) did was a beach cleanup. He must have been about 14 months old. At first, he just pointed out the trash for my husband and me to pick up; from there he progressed to picking it up himself. Since then, David has probably been on 12 to 15 beach cleanups and more than 30 volunteer projects. It has truly changed his life and his attitude on helping others. Now, whenever we are at the beach and he sees people leaving for the day and leaving their trash behind, he gets up and confronts them: How can they leave their trash? Who do they think is going to pick it up? Don't they know how it hurts the animals? Of course, the offenders immediately pick up their trash. What can they say to a child questioning them?

A few months ago, David was assigned a first-grade project in which he had to create a poster that was "all about David": his family, what he likes, what he doesn't like, and so on. He had to list three favorite things, which were Christmas, the zoo, and volunteering. This was with absolutely no prompting from me. I have proudly hung this poster in my office.

Lori Broadhurst
Florida

**My company, PricewaterhouseCoopers,** recently volunteered to help beautify Anacostia Park, the national park in Washington, D.C. For a day, hundreds of accountants, tax advisers, business process improvement analysts, and auditors traded their laptops and working papers for shovels, chain saws, and work gloves and descended upon the park. Working professionals from our D.C. metro office, who serve clients far and wide, participated in our firm's Month of Giving Campaign, in which every one of PwC's offices across the United States engaged in a community service activity during the month of June to show what an impact corporate volunteerism could have on our community. This was unique in that the effort was not a result of corporate social responsibility efforts meant to mitigate a negative community perception of our business, but rather a genuine attempt to help make a difference. I think that for me, the best part about the event was realizing just how many of my coworkers wanted to help benefit a community near us and lend a helping hand. Being part of an organization that is not only dedicated to delivering superior client service, but is also committed to contributing to the community, is very rewarding, and the event was a tangible representation of that belief. Some people say that if we all do a little, we can do a lot, and for that one day, a lot of us were committed to doing as much as we could collectively and seeing just what an impact we could make. Since that event, every time I take the bridge toward Anacostia, I look at the riverbed with pride, knowing that my firm and my coworkers cleared it, and then went back to business as normal the following day.

Andrew J. Hutsell
McLean, Virginia

**As a rookie volunteer,** I knew I didn't want to sit on the bench. So when I got the call to help Lou, a 91-year-old woman in need of housing repairs, I was eager to put my handyman skills to work. After that, I was hooked. Just a few months after discovering Make A Difference (www.makeadifference.org), I took on the role of project leader at a local domestic violence shelter and began to recruit volunteers to share the joy of reading with children.

My son, who is 11, also reads with the children at the shelter. I think this helps him as well as the clients. My son and I try to be positive role models for the kids in the shelter as well as for the mothers who have been victims of domestic violence.

In my first year as a reading buddy with Make A Difference, one of the students didn't know how to show respect to his teacher, and that was something we worked on the entire year. The greatest accomplishment for me was when he called her Mrs. Robinson rather than "teacher."

Lee Feldmeier
Phoenix, Arizona

**One of the most effective ways to recruit** is by personal invitation. A phone call works so much better than a piece of paper going home with all the kids, asking parents to help with a project. When the principal calls and says, "I need your help," it makes parents think, "Hey, someone needs me! They need *my* experience and skills."

George Theoaris
Des Moines, Iowa

## Voices of Change:
## Senator Elizabeth Dole

Several years ago, while I was preparing to begin my duties as president of the American Red Cross, my mother—who lived to be 102 years old and was always a source of inspiration for me—told me about her own experiences as a Red Cross volunteer during World War II. "Elizabeth," she said, "Nothing I ever did made me feel so important."

My mother showed me just how important it is to find a calling that infuses you with a sense of mission and passion. She taught me to search until you find something that makes you say, "Nothing I ever did made me feel so important."

I discovered that my calling was public service. The desire to help others and make our world a better place has driven me throughout my career. When I was president of the Red Cross, my focus was inspiring people to volunteer, to give of their financial resources, and to donate their blood. My position gave me a unique vantage point from which to view the world at its very best and its very worst. I have seen the evil humans can inflict on one another in the dim eyes of starving children in Somalia and in the paralyzing grief of parents in Oklahoma City. I have seen the monstrous destruction unleashed by nature in the rubble of neighborhoods laid waste by Hurricane Andrew.

I have felt the hopelessness and despair of families who have lost everything in a tornado's 260-mile-an-hour winds and terrifying violence.

No one can undo such grievous and unearned pain. But Red Cross volunteers make it their mission to bring compassion and caring to disaster victims. These remarkable people go wherever and whenever they are needed, providing emotional and practical support. And I can assure you, every one of them is grateful for the opportunity to serve.

Red Cross volunteers taught me about the durability of human hope and faith amid suffering. I've seen great hearts in tired bodies, driven past exhaustion to bring comfort to strangers. And I am grateful for these experiences.

In making your own contributions to this world, I hope that you, too, will consider a life of public service. You may not get rich in this calling, but you will enrich the lives of many. Your rewards will not be material, but rather the satisfaction of service—of making a positive difference in people's lives.

And when I say public service, I do not mean just running for office, but running a PTA meeting; I do not mean just serving in Congress, but serving food at a homeless shelter.

After all, whether on the floor of Congress, in the boardrooms of corporate America, or in the corridors of a big city hospital, there is no body of professional expertise and no anthology of case studies that can supplant the force of character.

Character provides both a sense of direction and a means to fulfillment. It asks not what you want to be, but who you want to be. For in the final analysis, it is your moral compass that counts for more than any bank balance or resume.

I hope that we all have lives as long and fulfilling as my mother's. And I hope that when we turn 102 and look back at our lives, it won't be the cars we drove or the titles we held or the awards we were given that we cherish the most. Instead, we will ask ourselves, "What did I stand for? Did I make a positive difference in the lives of others?" That is what truly matters in life.

*Senator Elizabeth Dole (North Carolina) has been named numerous times by the Gallup Poll as one of the world's 10 most admired women. Dole currently serves in a volunteer position as the National Director of Education and Information for Hospice.*

## Voices of Change:
## Danny Greene

A couple of years ago, 15 Home Depot stores in and around Charlotte, North Carolina, each offered $250 gift cards to help improve our communities. I was always looking for new partners with whom we could lend a helping hand, and someone mentioned the Shelter for Battered Women in Charlotte. I spoke with the director of the facility, and she actually laughed when she repeated my question: "Do we have any home improvement needs here? Please, come take a look."

I followed very secretive directions on a winding path to the unmarked, nondescript building that was a temporary home for approximately 25 women and their children. The door is always locked, and visitors are carefully screened before entering. One of the counselors, Wanda, was going to give me a tour of the facility, but first she made sure the coast was clear. The women staying there are usually in hiding and don't want to be seen, so she warned them that a man was coming through. These women had come from very abusive, sad situations.

As Wanda and I rounded the first corner, a woman who had not heard the warning came out of a bathroom and headed right toward me. Our eyes locked, and as if in slow motion, her head went down in shame. My heart dropped as I realized that she had a black eye, and the reality of the pain and despair at this place sank in. I went numb.

As I followed Wanda around, I just knew that this was the place for Team Depot. It wasn't so much the ugly colors on the walls, the dreary bathroom, the run-down playroom, or the old, worn carpeting. It was the heart of this shelter. We needed to be there to make it a better place, to brighten it up and somehow bring some joy to those women and those kids who might spend 30 days at a time there. I was able to get 11 of the gift cards, which meant that 76 Team Depot volunteers came out with a truckload of merchandise to "improve everything we touch." The gift cards took care of everything but the carpeting. We also landscaped, mulched, made a pavestone pathway, built a swing set, stained the kids' forts, donated a grill, and cooked lunch for everyone.

Most of the residents stayed hidden, but at the end of the day, several were seen sitting peacefully in the "memory garden" we created. It was a tremendous day for all of us.

Recently, the parent company of the shelter, United Family Services, held a "Men for Change" breakfast. I was thrilled to present the shelter with a Home Depot CommUnity Impact Grant for $7,800 for their new carpeting. My Team Depot experience at the Shelter for Battered Women opened my eyes to a very sad element of our society: domestic violence, the least-reported crime in America and one that occurs once every nine seconds. This is unacceptable, and as a trainer at The Home Depot, I take advantage of my opportunity to share our respect policy with new hires. I talk about character and integrity and doing the right thing. In my own small way, I hope to make an impact in my community by promoting healthy attitudes and relationships.

*Danny Greene is a trainer at The Home Depot and is part of Team Depot, the employee volunteer program. As District Team Depot Captain, he sits on the first Team Depot Community Council.*

## Voices of Change:
## Charles (Chuck) Turlinski

"

For 35 years, I have been in an industry that has manufacturers all over the globe. Much of my travel is to developing countries. I've witnessed much poverty and the unfortunate results of being unable to provide for oneself and one's family. Most of my volunteer and philanthropic work support self-sufficiency through commercial development. What most of the people in the developing world want is the opportunity to provide for themselves—much more than aid. Jobs not only provide income, but they also provide self-esteem, self-respect, and environments that reduce disease. Jobs are the building blocks of an environment that can support its inhabitants. Jobs provide the basis for education to sustain and nurture continued development.

I met a very successful manufacturer who lived in Hong Kong. He had a beautiful home high on a hill overlooking the ocean in Phuket, Thailand. From his balcony, a long way down the beach, he could see the local fishermen bring in their boats before sunset. There were hundreds of boats in the native fleet. The fishermen were poor by most standards, but they were rich by the standard of the local population. These men owned their own boats and provided well for their families. They lived in one- or two-room homes, but the biggest asset was their boats. An apprentice fisherman would have to work 10 years or more to own a boat, if he was lucky and talented.

One day, everything in their lives changed. On December 26, 2005, the sea receded and the boats that were not already out to sea, were now hundreds of yards from the water's edge. Most of the old men knew what this meant: tsunami. They alerted the population and fled to higher ground. These were the lucky ones; they survived. When they returned, their village was devastated: no shacks, no houses, no crops, and most critically, no boats.

My friend knew what the result would be. For life to go on, these people needed to bury the dead, mourn, and rebuild, but most important, they needed to return to the sea. Without their boats, they did not have the means to rebuild their lives. My friend took it upon himself to replace the fleet of boats lost that day in December 2005. His goal was to provide 100 boats, each with a small motor and all fishing gear; that way the fishermen could be productive the day the boats launched.

He mobilized business contacts all over the world. The world was shocked by the tsunami and support was immediate. In two months, he had raised the funds for 103 boats (five of which my company sponsored).

The scars left by the tsunami will not be forgotten in this generation or the next. But the ability for life to go on for 103 families was restored by one man's compassion and tenacity.

Jai Waney has inspired me in many ways, but this was one of the most vivid examples of how one individual can affect the lives of hundreds for years to come, through one act of compassion.

*Charles (Chuck) Turlinski is CEO of the The Limited, a division of Limited Brands. He serves on the President's Council on Service and Civic Participation, which is administered by the Corporation for National & Community Service and was established to recognize the important contributions Americans of all ages are making within their communities through service and civic engagement. Over the past three years, the President's Council has recognized more than 300,000 Americans with the President's Volunteer Service Award. To learn how your organization could earn a President's Volunteer Service Award, visit www.presidentialserviceawards.com.*

ONE OF THE BEST EXAMPLES of infectious engagement that I know is a volunteer named Juanita Seace, who worked with Hands On Atlanta for 16 years as a volunteer leader. She enthusiastically led dozens of service projects for old and young people, friends, and acquaintances. She embodied commitment: "When people find out that I'm 74 and I'm still volunteering, they think, 'Gee—I can do that too.'" She was a quiet leader: "We don't have to lead by being out front, but we all have to lead by example, and volunteering is a great way to inspire others." Juanita recently passed away, and her funeral was a tribute to her profound impact and deeply embraced passion for engaging her community. Her friends laughed at all the times she had "persuaded" them to join her at service projects. "Volunteering is a good way of meeting people," Juanita said. "I don't think I'd know many people from outside my community and social circles if I wasn't involved in service through Hands On Atlanta. It's a wonderful way of keeping in touch with the community. I enjoy connecting with people of diverse backgrounds. To me, volunteering is the next best thing to travel." What kind of world would it be if we all traveled on life's journey equipped with Juanita's compassion and curiosity?

M.N.

# CHAPTER 6

# Duty, honor, country

## CITIZENSHIP AND POLITICAL ACTION

OVER THE LAST 40 YEARS, we have seen a precipitous drop in civic participation—in voting, reading the newspaper, and writing to our representatives. This is dangerous for our nation. It enfeebles our democratic system and leaves us ill-equipped to solve the serious challenges that we face domestically and internationally. We have lost the idea that our government and our leaders are extensions of ourselves and that we can shape the course of our nation and our world.

We sometimes lose sight of the radical proposition of democracy; that each of us has inalienable rights and responsibilities. The idea of our American democracy was envisioned as a "City on a Hill," but it has taken enormous personal sacrifice and leadership to establish such ideals as a woman's right to vote, or of all people to be free and full citizens under the law."

# BE THE CHANGE!

Systemic change often necessitates working through the processes of local, state, and federal government. This can be overwhelming, but as the following stories suggest, individuals underestimate their power to make a difference. A few letters can change the course of action on a local issue. A strong presence at a few city council meetings can ensure that a change is enacted. Ultimately, our democracy works extraordinarily well. Our leaders will, largely, follow their constituencies. That gives each of us an enormous power.

The stories in this chapter tell us to be patient. Policy change may take a longer time and be more indirect. It means going to meetings, rallying others, and working through systems and processes. But these efforts can alleviate critical needs over the long term. Poverty among seniors has been reduced by millions in our nation as a result of Social Security and Medicare; millions of acres of wild land have been preserved for future generations; and we can count on clean water and safe foods—all as a result of the work of ordinary citizens working in concert with lawmakers who have created legislative change.

The inspiring lesson of the following stories is that ordinary citizens can make an enormous difference by exercising their voice and voting, helping inform and educate the populace around issues, and by offering up their own skills as public servants. It is up to us to reclaim and renew our democracy every day. Ensuring a strong democracy is not the province of history, it is the responsibility of each of us.

**Voting is very important to me.** African Americans were murdered, lynched, maimed, burned out of their homes, beaten, and jailed for my right to vote in this country. For me, not to vote would be a crime against my forefathers.

I owe a lot to my ancestors and those who helped them. I try to give back by being conscious of whom I support. If I don't feel good about a candidate, I won't vote for them. Voting is too important for me to take it lightly.

Kristen Yolas
Sherman Oaks, California

> Capitol Advantage is a private, nonpartisan company specializing in facilitating civic participation. For more information, visit www.congress.org.

**A few letters can make a big difference.** I work on the city council, representing a half million people. But if just 30 people write me about the same issue, I will notice that. People underestimate their representative's willingness to talk to them and take on projects.

About a year ago, one of our city commissions approved a landfill expansion project without giving public notice of the meeting. When some citizens later found out, 10 of them complained. As a result, the decision was reversed and we changed the system of public notice. We now have a Web site and other ways to make sure the community never misses another meeting. This was all from just 10 people speaking up!

C. David Briley
Nashville, Tennessee

**Do something with your voice.** The passion that comes through when you yell at the TV matters; voting matters; talking to your neighbors about why you're supporting a county councilman matters. Write a letter to the TV station thanking it for running a story about a political hearing or community meeting. Let people know about your community passion, and change really can happen.

Lisa Danielson
Seattle, Washington

For fast facts and information on HIV/AIDS across the world, visit www.global healthfacts.org.

**I am a part of the Kidz Commission on AIDS.** Recently, we went to New York's City Hall to protest and demand better education on AIDS and HIV in New York City schools. I've learned that if you want it, you've got to go and get it. The government can't read your mind, and it sure isn't going to jump right up and do it, either. Sometimes it takes a little bit of courage and willpower to go from little dog all the way to top dog.

Jolynda Jenkins
Bronx, New York

**Community responsibility can begin young.** Once we adults painted and repaired a playground at a school. We involved the kids by instituting a "Peaceful Playgrounds" program. After all, the playground is really their community. For example, the younger kids were in charge of keeping the playground clean and for reporting graffiti. Responsible kids are usually better-behaved kids.

George Theoaris
Des Moines, Iowa

**There are so many cultural** and financial divisions in our current society. Service is a vehicle to address those problems. It makes you knowledgeable about, and sympathetic to, the challenges other people face.

For instance, in the military, the team can be an unusual mix: You have a surfer boy from California, an Italian from New York City, and a black guy from Chicago. But they're all bonding, and all identifying together as Americans. Service can be bonding in the same way.

John Gomperts
Washington, D.C.

**I usually like to focus on the particulars** of an issue, but sometimes you need to reach for the universal. I've been acting as a ringleader for folks in the neighborhood who are fighting the city park board, which is trying to give away public parkland for a private school to use for athletic fields. The park board superintendent has been trying to shut down discussion of the issue.

"The inability of those in power to still the voices of their own consciences is the great force leading to change."
Kenneth Kaunda

We set up booths where we could explain the issue to people, and we got hundreds of them to sign our petitions. It was really invigorating to see what people can do when they join together. At the end, though, I felt a little let down and wondered, why am I doing all this? I mean, there's a war on—why am I fighting these piddly local issues? But then I thought about the larger themes involved, like free speech, and I decided those issues aren't too shabby.

Chris Steller
Minneapolis, Minnesota

# BE THE CHANGE!

In the early 1970s, I was a newly elected senator serving on the Armed Services Committee. Senator Stennis, our committee chairman, asked me, as a new member, to go over to West Germany, spend two or three weeks with NATO, and then submit a report to the committee.

One of the things I focused on was the storage and deployment sites for our tactical nuclear weapons. It is important to keep in mind that this was shortly after the Vietnam War, when the mood and morale of the U.S. military was somewhat comparable to the present mood and morale of the Russian military. I remember very well visiting with U.S. generals who explained to me that all of our tactical nuclear weapons were secure. Everything was wonderful. There was no problem. After one of those briefings, as I was leaving an area where tactical nuclear weapons were stored, I shook hands with a sergeant and felt a piece of folded paper pressed into my hand, which I slipped into my pocket. When I had an opportunity, I looked at the paper. The sergeant had written, "Senator Nunn, please meet me at the barracks around 6:00 tonight. I have very important information for you."

Having been an enlisted man myself, I knew I'd better find out what the sergeant had in mind. So I went to the meeting. He and three or four of his fellow sergeants related a horror story: a story of a demoralized military; a story of drug and alcohol abuse; a story of U.S. soldiers actually guarding nuclear weapons while they were stoned on drugs. The story went on for more than two hours. I came out of that session thoroughly shaken and determined to do something.

When I returned to Washington, I went directly to see then-Secretary of Defense James Schlessinger and told him that we had a real problem in Germany. I related to him how the soldiers guarding our tactical nuclear missiles felt that it would take no more than a group of six to eight well-trained terrorists to gain control over one of our tactical nuclear compounds in the middle of western Europe. Such an incident, even if it lasted only a few hours, would have had a devastating effect on European public opinion. So we had a major problem, one that grew out of the psychological trauma of the Vietnam War, and it was not being acknowledged. Secretary Schlessinger saw to it that steps were taken, in the next few months and over the next few years, to remedy the situation.

In the early fall of 1991, just after Soviet president Mikhail Gorbachev was released from house arrest following a failed coup in the Soviet Union, I was on an official visit to Moscow and met with him in his Kremlin office. This time I knew enough to ask him directly if he had retained command and control of the Soviet nuclear forces during the coup attempt. President Gorbachev did not answer. That was answer enough.

Over the next two months, I formed a partnership with Senator Richard Lugar that eventually led to the Nunn-Lugar Cooperative Threat Reduction Program, which helped the states of the former Soviet Union secure and destroy their weapons of mass destruction and cope with the challenges related to these weapons, including assistance in gainfully employing literally thousands of former Soviet scientists.

At the beginning, the Nunn-Lugar proposal was greeted with opposition from most of our colleagues. However, we worked diligently day by day with key senators, and many others, and finally convinced Congress that this expenditure (to assist our former enemy) was essential for our own security.

Since 1991, the United States, Russia, and the former Soviet Union working together have deactivated or destroyed 6,670 nuclear warheads as well as hundreds of missiles, launchers, bombers, submarines, and test tunnels, without a shot being fired in anger. The Nunn-Lugar program also helped achieve the removal of all strategic nuclear warheads from Ukraine, Kazakhstan, and Belarus. Three nations voluntarily removed their fingers from the nuclear trigger, and today's world would be far different if that had not happened.

We sometimes think that issues of nuclear war and terrorism are beyond the province of ordinary citizens or even our leaders. Lawmakers have a mandate to be creative and far-sighted in preventing nuclear disaster. And ordinary citizens have an obligation to hold our leaders accountable. Our future depends on it.

*Senator Sam Nunn is cochairman and CEO of the Nuclear Threat Initiative, a charitable organization working to reduce the global threats from nuclear, biological, and chemical weapons. He served as a United States Senator from Georgia for 24 years (1972–1996). Senator Nunn and Senator Richard Lugar were nominated for Nobel Peace Prizes in 2000 and 2001 for their work in conceiving, legislating, and sustaining this important program.*

# BE THE CHANGE!

**During my time as an advocate** with the Georgia state legislature, I learned how a little action goes a long way. State legislators will tell you that five (five!) letters from constituents on an issue constitutes a "landslide" of support or opposition.

Margaret Hall
Boston, Massachusetts

The Army, Navy, and Marine Corps were established in 1775, in concurrence with the American Revolution. The Department of the Navy and the U.S. Coast Guard were founded in 1798. To learn more about the armed services, visit www.defenselink.mil.

**I know a group of young homeless people** who live in a facility that helps them make the transition into adulthood. One day they heard that their insurance benefits were going to be slashed. They got involved: They went to rallies, they wrote letters, and one of them even met with the governor. They knew that they could be part of the solution.

Hal Cato
Nashville, Tennessee

**I was talking to an activist in a Hispanic community.** He pointed out that his neighborhood had a lot of the same concerns as any Anglo neighborhood: streetlights, potholes, and safety for their kids. Yet they weren't able to express those concerns as well as their Anglo neighbors. The city council meetings are set so that you come in, sign in, sit down, and, once you're called, have 45 seconds to make your statement. If English is your second language, it's much tougher to express yourself clearly in 45 seconds. The system isn't set up to hear out non-English speakers. We can change that, it's fixable. We just have to do it!

Lisa Danielson
Seattle, Washington

**If people want to see change,** they should get out and get involved in the community rather than wait for someone to make a change for them. There was a group of people in the Grant Park neighborhood that got together and said they wanted a really good public school for the kids. So they worked for several years and created a charter school for the neighborhood. The parents got together and said, "We really want to have a hand in education." And they did!

Beth Fenger
Atlanta, Georgia

> "This country will not be a good place for any of us to live in unless we make it a good place for all of us to live in."
> Theodore Roosevelt

**I volunteer because it is my way of giving back** to my great community and the best country in the world. This great nation has given me more opportunities and blessings than I could have possibly hoped for anywhere else. I was born an Iowa farm boy and became a professional USDA soil scientist, attending several fine universities—where else but in America? Yes, many things need improving, but who better to do that than me and you and all of us who have been so richly blessed? It is an honor to be able to volunteer and give back a small part of what we have been allowed to earn.

Bill Pauls
Columbia, Missouri

**Local politicians like to be kept informed** all of the time, not just when a vote concerning budgets is pending. Make yourself a familiar face at all commission meetings, and share your appreciation of their job frequently. You will find that you will have a much friendlier reception when the time comes to ask for something.

Judi Reynolds
Decatur, Tennessee

## Voices of Change: Cokie Roberts

My family was heavily involved in politics. And when that's the case, it's all about serving the community. You were considered an employee of the public. My parents gave back to the community, and that's what we were expected to do, too. Then I went to a Catholic school, where I also had an obligation to serve the community. It was part of my entire period of growing up. It was taught with reading, writing, and arithmetic, and fed with grits and bacon.

That's what our family life was—going around to events, talking about people's problems, being involved in civil rights when it was wildly unpopular. I never considered not being involved. That would have been to opt out of the entire ethos. That would be the definition of an ingrate.

And as I became an adult, it was a part of who I was. After many years, I achieved a certain degree of visibility in my work. As a reporter and commentator, I always felt I was doing a good thing, helping people make judgment calls as voters. I felt that I was doing something that mattered, and I wasn't just lying around, popping bonbons into my mouth. But then I decided to be more personally involved, and I very consciously decided to devote more of my time to public service. I thought, "OK, now I have to spend most of the rest of my life involved in this."

At that point, I resigned from my *This Week* position at ABC, and I called Save the Children and said, "I want to get involved with you." Now I serve as vice chair of the organization, I serve on other nonprofit boards, and I spend time in the community. And I try to get Congress to behave as well. It was a conscious decision for me.

In particular, I try to get young people involved in civic engagement. You can certainly help individuals, and that is work to do. But politics is where you can change the laws and culture. Civic engagement is your birthright, and one that women and minorities worked hard to achieve. If you get involved on this level, you can see the effect of lasting change.

Public service is unbelievably rewarding. I was in Kashmir after the 2005 Pakistan earthquake, talking to a little girl up in the mountains; she had never gone to school. We talked about how that would change her life. It's these kinds of incredible experiences that make it so rewarding. I don't think anybody ever feels as good as they do when they're helping other people. When you sit down and think: What really makes me happy? That's the answer. I don't mean that in a namby-pamby way. I mean it's almost selfish, when you get that much joy from helping other people.

I was recently at a function with Sandra Day O'Connor. She was talking to a group of kids, and one child was telling her how he had come from a poor family and didn't feel like he had a lot of opportunities. And Sandra said, "Look, I was raised on a ranch in Texas and ended up in Stanford and on the Supreme Court. I did what no one else expected me to do." This boy came over to her the next day and knelt by her side—which took a lot of courage to do—and said, "I just want you to know that because of what you said, I'm going to go for it." She burst into tears, she was so moved. Who knows what effect one thing you say or do might have on someone else?

St. Francis said, "Preach always; sometimes use words."

*Cokie Roberts serves as a senior news analyst for NPR, where she was the congressional correspondent for more than 10 years. In addition to her work for NPR, Roberts is a political commentator for ABC News, serving as an on-air analyst for the network. She was the first broadcast journalist to win the highly prestigious Everett McKinley Dirksen Award for coverage of Congress. Roberts is the recipient of numerous other broadcasting awards, including a 1991 Emmy for her contribution to the ABC News special, "Who Is Ross Perot?"*

**I am a World War II veteran,** and I donate my time talking to local high school students about the war and my experiences with it. I do it because I want the kids to understand the reality of the war beyond what they can learn in their textbooks. And I want to be able to tell my story.

I love when I can see that I have captured their attention! I especially love it when they ask me lots of questions after I'm done speaking, because then I know that they were really listening and interested in what I was saying. I think I perform a very valuable civic service by doing this.

Ralph Herron
Watts Flats, New York

**Even when you don't "win,"** being politically active is one of the most important activities you can do. The ability to even *be* politically active is one of the greatest rights afforded to Americans.

Catherine Bassett
Somerville, Massachusetts

**Good leaders don't recognize the status quo.** They don't think about how things are and how they've always been done. They think about what needs to change.

Lisa Danielson
Seattle, Washington

**The National Alliance for Public Charter Schools** increases the number of high-performing charter schools available to all families, particularly low-income and minority families who don't have access to quality public schools. Visit www.public charters.org to learn more.

**Tell a politician or someone** who is a leader in the community that you recognize they are doing a good job. Then thank them!

Michelle Demain
Atlanta, Georgia

**One of the most underappreciated ways** to serve one's community is to work within the federal government. Many times, people think about the government in terms of how it can be influenced. But why not try to serve the community from inside one of the most powerful entities, instead of just trying to exert external influence on it? That's why I work with the Partnership for Public Service, whose official goal is to "make the government an employer of choice for talented, dedicated Americans through educational outreach, research, legislative advocacy, and hands-on partnerships with agencies on workforce management issues."

Max Stier
Washington, D.C.

**Don't give up.** It takes a lot of small acts to see end results. I am a Green Party member. I write to free political prisoners and lobby for saving the redwoods. It's all part of my personal philosophy of being environmentally aware and an active member of a community. I have learned through these experiences that change is possible.

Michele Mician
Sarasota, Florida

**Changing incorrect perceptions or acts** must be done in a reasonable way so that change is accomplished willingly. If you can get people to "do the right thing" and still not be turned off, you have accomplished your objective. For example, I once saw a group catching crabs all day. They were having a wonderful day at the shore. I looked at the crabs and knew that over half of them were illegal—way too small.

So I showed them how to pick up a crab without being pinched, then asked them to check the size against the ruler. They made the determination themselves that half were too small. When I left they thanked me and even shook my hand!

Don Winslow
Ocean Pines, Maryland

**When you volunteer on a committee** (like I do with the local planning commission), you can't expect to see sweeping changes in your town based on the work you are doing. You have to take pride in each little difference that you can make. For instance, there was an old garage in one part of town that was a total eyesore. But the owners refused to tear it down or fix it up. I was part of the group that drafted a new comprehensive plan that forced the owners to make changes. Again, it doesn't seem like a big deal. But to the people who live in that area it was. You have to be willing to win these fights one little skirmish at a time.

Allison Dupree
Jamestown, New York

The Partnership for Public Service works to make the government an employer of choice for talented, dedicated Americans through educational outreach, research, legislative advocacy, and hands-on partnerships with agencies on workforce management issues. For more information, visit www.ourpublic service.org.

# BE THE CHANGE!

**I volunteered with Election Protection in Ohio** for the 2004 presidential election. I saw firsthand the problems that the media casually wrote off. It was raining, and our polling location did not have stair railings for the elderly voters, who constituted the majority of our voting group. The parking lot was not large enough for the cars, and the police were ticketing the cars parked at the curb. Hundreds of voters came with postcards showing they were registered, but were turned away because they were told they were at the wrong voting location. Yet the postcards they carried had the location clearly printed on the front, and it was correct. I was devastated after this experience.

I work with organizations to make sure that this situation does not happen again. I am working to make public the inadequate situations for physically challenged voters. I plan to work with the county to make changes to allow voters to confirm their valid registration prior to Election Day. If we don't work to make changes, our votes will never count.

P. L. Gray
Cleveland, Ohio

*"In every community there is work to be done. In every nation, there are wounds to heal. In every heart, there is the power to do it."*
Marianne Williamson

**Through volunteering,** I've learned to accept and work with others. I've learned that no matter how much you want to protest and scream, the real activism and volunteering sometimes comes down to getting other people aware of what's going on.

Ashley Oesterle
West Caldwell, New Jersey

# To the Rescue!
# Volunteering for Disaster Relief

**I point out to people that despite disaster** and crisis needs—like 9/11 or the tsunami—there are other needs that have to be met too. For example, after 9/11, volunteers were not needed at the site because so many people had already come forward. But the homeless still needed help, food shelters still needed servers, children in foster care still needed attention. They were still there.

Allan Sih
New York, New York

**I was a graduate student living** in Mexico City during the 1985 earthquake. When it hit, all of the infrastructure, such as the police and medical facilities, were caught off guard. So the neighborhoods took over, forming brigades and directing traffic. All of downtown was in rubble, and people were digging through it with their bare hands. People didn't sit around and wait for organized help; they instinctively took care of it. Eventually, the police, the army, and the foreign rescue teams showed up, but the local people were the first on the scene.

Andrew Leone
Fort Lauderdale, Florida

# BE THE CHANGE!

**I cannot ever describe** the devastation and the hurt in my heart seeing homes destroyed, barges lifted out of the Gulf only to land on the other side of the street on top of hotels and homes. This experience has certainly humbled me to the point that those sights and the people that I talked to will forever be embedded in my mind.

Sharon
Edmonds, Washington

**What I really love about service** is that it is an "engine of goodwill." People from all over the U.S.A. (and some from abroad) converged in Biloxi, Mississippi, with the simple goal of helping others. All these kindred spirits pack a lot of energy, which easily grows and spreads in this environment. The recipients of the volunteer work of course experience and internalize the goodwill, but the volunteers do too.

Erik
Warrenville, Illinois

**A few of the houses** that we helped with were still wet, still hadn't been cleared of personal belongings and had a stench that brought me to my knees. I decided to take a break after the third day of gutting and hit the streets to do some community outreach. I came to find out quickly that listening to some of the neighbors' stories and seeing the looks in their eyes were as emotionally taxing as the physicality of ripping a stranger's home apart.

Shannon
Edmonds, Washington

**On New Year's Eve** I was standing on a back street of Biloxi. There were no lights on, no people around. I looked around and saw the stacks of branches, the piles of trash, the gutted houses. I was with a volunteer from Dartmouth College, and we looked at each other and both knew that there was no place on earth we'd rather be. How weird. I thought about "why" for a long time. And then it occurred to me: I was standing in hope. The trash was in piles. The houses were gutted. The street I'd just walked down was clear. Hope. I was standing in it, and it was everywhere.

"Monkey" Mike
Los Angeles, California

# BE THE CHANGE!

**I was first affected by service** when I volunteered to work with the Appalachia Service Project in eighth grade. I continued to work with them through high school and then college, when I served as summer staff each year. I essentially grew up with that organization, and it was truly a powerful experience for me. Prior to working with them, I was not familiar with that region and had no idea of the extent of rural poverty that we have in this nation. I couldn't comprehend that there are families who do not have running water or electricity.

I began to feel a little discouraged about my service work when I became a staff member during college. At that point, I could understand more of the dynamics of our service, as well as some of the shortcomings of short-term mission work. Sometimes volunteering can be so "volunteer powered" that it disenfranchises the community it is trying to serve. Many people volunteer for the feeling that you get after completing an act of kindness. But we can fix houses until we are blue in the face. If a person is hungry, we give him food. But we should be asking ourselves, "Why is this person going hungry in the wealthiest nation in the world?" We need to know how to ask the bigger questions rather than just address the symptoms. That's the difference, I believe, between justice and charity. We need to embrace education and advocacy around those bigger issues in order to effect change.

Rev. Amanda Hendler-Voss
Atlanta, Georgia

> "Each time a person stands up for an ideal, or acts to improve the lot of others, he sends forth a tiny ripple of hope, and crossing each other from a million different centers of energy and daring, those ripples build a current that can sweep down the mightiest walls of oppression and resistance."
> Robert F. Kennedy

## Voices of Change: Soumaya Khalifa

I WAS BORN IN EGYPT, and my family and I—who are of Muslim and Arab descent—moved to Texas when I was a child. It was not until I came to the United States that I realized the differences between black and white or Muslim and Christian. I was not comfortable in many situations relating to religion because most others were Christian, so I learned to show parts of myself to different people at different times. I lived my entire life from my teens to early adulthood only showing parts of myself to the world. I was not comfortable letting others know I was Muslim until about 15 years ago.

Now, I want to let the world know that Muslims are a part of the American culture. There are more than 7 million Muslims across the United States, and most of us are subject to many misconceptions. I decided that I wanted to do something in terms of outreach. I wanted to make the community better and have Muslims become more accepted. I thought the best way to do this would be through education. I became affiliated with the Islamic Networks Group, out of California's Bay Area. We go out in front of audiences that are mainly made up of Christians and Jews to talk about misconceptions, and we hold teacher workshops and law enforcement workshops, helping people better understand the Muslim community and help us have a better quality of life. We now have 30 volunteers trained as speakers who go out to different organizations to have conversations, conduct workshops, and help people overcome their phobias related to race, gender, and religion.

This has been a phenomenal movement. Although our initial reception was mixed, most people realize that this is long overdue and much needed. My ultimate vision is that people will connect with each other as fellow human beings and put aside any differences they might have with each other. I hope that the day will come soon when people learn to embrace each other's differences and learn from them. Tolerance and acceptance are key to making changes in our world.

*Soumaya Khalifa founded the Islamic Speakers Bureau of Georgia in 2001 with the goal of educating the Atlanta community about Islam and Muslims through guest speakers and workshops. To learn more, visit www.isbatlanta.org.*

# Voices of Change:
# Senator Bill Frist

As someone who took up public life as a second vocation, I'm often asked, "Why would a successful surgeon want to become a senator?" It's simple. When you boil it down to its essence, medicine exists to improve the life of another human being. Public service exists to serve the best interests of the citizen. Thus, the underlying motivation for surgeons and senators is exactly the same.

However, I learned long ago that some vehicles allow us a greater reach than others. As a physician, I was able to help one person at a time. As a senator, I can work to help millions of Americans—in Tennessee and across the nation—whom I could never serve on a one-to-one basis. But there's more to life than public service. There's also private service. And I've tried to continue to use my medical skills to help others in a private way.

In July 2000, I spent six days in Africa on a medical mission trip, during which public and private service intersected for me. We visited six hospitals in three countries, eventually ending up in southern Sudan, a stop not originally on our agenda and a country that is being wracked by a brutal civil war. As we unloaded the airplane, we were greeted by hundreds of people singing and cheering our arrival. From there we were led to an abandoned schoolhouse that served as a hospital for the next four days. There, we operated from early morning until late at night in one of the most primitive settings I have ever seen. There was no running water. No electricity. No anesthesia. One patient walked 62 miles to get there. He was carried part of the way.

The evening before we left, I was called to see a patient who had asked to see "the American doctor." I walked into the room, where he was lying with a big smile on his face, despite the fact that he had just lost his left leg and two fingers. We talked, and the smile remained. He told me that two years before, his wife and two children had been murdered during the war. Just eight days before, he had lost his leg and fingers to a land mine.

Finally I asked, "How can you be smiling?"

"Because I believe in Jesus Christ," he replied, "and because you are the American doctor."

In the transplant world, I'm accustomed to people thanking me for replacing a heart or a lung, but not because I'm American. I said, "What do you mean?"

And he replied that everything he had lost—his family, his leg, his fingers—would be worth it if he could just enjoy what we have in America: freedom. His desire for freedom enabled him to endure all that befell him.

Sudan may seem an unusual place to be reminded of the freedoms we take for granted in America, but the lesson I learned from that hopeful patient is just one of the rewards I gained from the mission trip. I set out to provide aid to those in desperate need of medical care but ended up being inspired and educated by the very patients I sought to help.

That's the way of service, both public and private. The rewards often far exceed expectations.

*U.S. Senate Majority Leader Bill Frist, M.D. was the first practicing physician to be elected to the Senate since 1928. Dr. Frist is particularly passionate about confronting the global AIDS pandemic. He frequently takes medical mission trips to Africa to perform surgery on and care for those in need, and he strives to continue to raise awareness about the HIV/AIDS crisis throughout the world.*

## Voices of Change: Sandra Day O'Connor

I grew up on a remote ranch where there were no opportunities for public service. When I went to Stanford, I became involved in a number of activities at the university as a volunteer. Part of the reason was so I could get to know other students, but I enjoyed it, and I became good at it.

After I married, my husband was sent to Germany. I followed him, and we lived there for more than three years. I worked as a civilian attorney for the Quartermaster Market Center, and I met a German woman who was my mother's age. She was one of the few people I met in Germany who was engaged in public service. She would help refugees from the East Zone— mothers coming across with small children—find places to live and jobs. I would go with her once a week. I was trying to learn German, and she would speak to me in German as she did her volunteer work. I thought that in a country where volunteer work was not the norm, she was making a real difference.

My husband and I talked about staying on in Europe. Both of us had developed the notion that we wanted to be involved in the community. Wherever we lived, we wanted to find a place where, through volunteer service, we would become acquainted with the community, be a part of the process there, and create the environment we wanted to live in.

We came back to the United States and found a place where each of us could be involved: Phoenix, Arizona. It was the political and economic capital of Arizona, and people from everywhere lived there. My husband and I became involved in activities for the community. I became president of the Junior League of Phoenix. Its whole purpose is getting young women involved in community service. We would introduce countless women to volunteer opportunities and get them involved in community service.

Helping others makes you feel good about yourself. But it has a broader purpose. You can be a part of shaping your community in ways that you think are better. Find an organization that is doing work in an area of interest to you. Get so deeply involved that you are an influential part of what the organization is doing.

*Sandra Day O'Connor, the first woman to be appointed to the United States Supreme Court, serving from 1981 to 2006, is renowned for her political independence and pragmatic decisions. As a moderate conservative on a polarized court, she often cast the swing vote on contentious issues. Prior to her nomination to the Supreme Court, O'Connor served in Arizona as assistant attorney general, trial judge, state senator, and member of the Arizona Court of Appeals.*

# REFLECTIONS

WORKING AT A SOUP KITCHEN, tutoring children, building homes—these are all powerful ways of making a difference. But my experience in working with thousands of volunteers has taught me that soon we all begin to question the systemic issues that we are trying to address through hands-on service. Why are the children that we are tutoring so far behind in their academic development? What kind of treatment options do the homeless men we are working with at the shelter have if they have addiction problems? Why is there so little affordable housing for families that are working hard in necessary but low-wage jobs?

One of our Hands On volunteers came up with the idea of creating a platform for groups to pose these questions and search for answers. We launched the Citizen Academy initiative, which started with volunteer faculty leading discussion groups on issues of homelessness, on how to start and lead your own service project, and on civil-rights bus tours tracing the student movement in the South and sharing the lessons of the movement for generations coming of age today.

The idea caught fire around the country. Soon there were TeamWorks programs in San Francisco that brought people together over a period of months to serve and then gather to share ideas about specific issues like HIV prevention and services. In Philadelphia, leadership forums bring people together to talk about citizen and service leadership and create networks for change.

What if all of us felt equipped to change our society? The opportunity is there.

M.N.

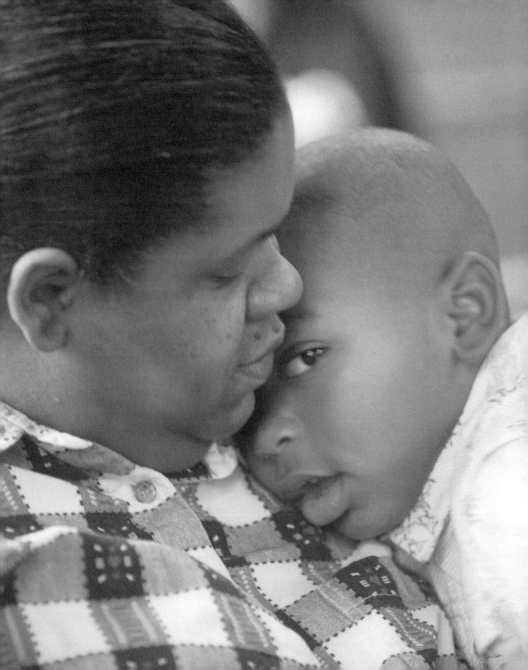

# CHAPTER 7

# A personal transformation
## THE CHANGE CIRCLES BACK TO YOU

WITHOUT DOUBT, THE MOST COMMON refrain that I hear from people who are engaged in helping others is "Service helped me more than those I was helping." Volunteering, serving, taking action to make a difference is perhaps the most important form of self-help that our world offers. Service has been recognized across traditions and time as the best antidote to despair. It offers a way to bring balance to our solipsistic and materialist culture. Truly, it offers hope. As contributor Krystyna Elizabeth Bublick says, "There is no better exercise for the soul than reaching down and lifting a child close to your heart."

The stories in this chapter offer a glimpse into the multifaceted personal returns on the investment of service. We see people discover new friends, cultures, parts of town, and skills. Many find their professional or vocational calling in the process of volunteering. Some report that volunteering helps them keep their moral balance, overcome fears and personal tragedies, and renew their appreciation for life.

Several contributors relate that in striving to be a role model for others, they discovered their own best selves. "By positively helping others we are constantly constructing ourselves." We also discover our own power—we overcome hopelessness and frustration and find our own personal ability to change things.

Perhaps most fundamentally, being in service cultivates our empathy. By allowing us to walk in the shoes of another, empathy breeds compassion, patience, and perspective. It gives us renewed appreciation for the blessings of our own lives. It can help heal our own broken places.

**Volunteering helps me get back** to being the good person I know I am. With all the temptations out there in the world, it is easy to get lost, especially living on a college campus. Volunteering gets me back on track and reminds me of my morals and values.

Lori Hobson
Ypsilanti, Michigan

**I signed up for my first volunteer** experience for all of the wrong reasons: I thought the group leader was cute. However, the power of the experience overtook my initial intention, and I came out of my week of service a changed person.

The turning point for me was the night I spent as a hospitality minister at a drop-in center for homeless men. I arrived expecting to serve sandwiches and coffee to a "bunch of bums." Instead, I spent the evening with a group of very intelligent, interesting, and valuable human beings who also happened to be homeless. I volunteered at that drop-in center for the remainder of my college career, and after college my first job was as a housing case manager for people transitioning from shelters into permanent housing.

Jeannie McNab
Seattle, Washington

**Community service changed me** because it made me realize that my life is not my own. There is so much more to this world than me. It's a humbling experience to realize that you are not the center of the universe.

Rebekah Lightfoot
Waldo, Arkansas

**I was assigned to arrange and manage** basketball games with ex-convicts in transitional housing. I was very nervous at first. These guys were all nonviolent offenders, in their late 20s to early 30s. Why would they respect me, a young, white goofball from the suburbs? But I took on the job because it was something that made me nervous, and I really wanted to stretch myself. It ended up being a very rewarding service project. I can't say I made any really great friends there, but I got to know these guys as just guys, and not ex-cons.

Derek Darling
Rochester, New York

**In high school, I was in a choir** that performed upbeat, slightly cheesy song-and-dance numbers to large audiences. One time we visited a hospice during the Christmas season to perform for kids with terminal cancer. For me, the days leading up to this visit were depressing. I couldn't think of anything worse than a dying child experiencing what would probably be a final holiday. However, I put aside these thoughts as I sang and danced to songs like "'Twas the Night Before Christmas" and "The Christmas Song."

Before I knew it, I was genuinely enjoying myself. Watching these kids smile, laugh, and sing along with me and my friends during what was probably the worst time in their lives humbled me. I saw that their spirits were bright and beautiful, even though their bodies had failed them. Being a witness to that has changed how I feel about each and every Christmas I'm blessed to experience. Now, instead of worrying about what I'm receiving or how much money I'll be able to save, I always remember how brave those kids were, and how a simple song made them smile and be thankful for the lives they were still holding on to.

Erica Starks
Indianapolis, Indiana

**My first volunteer experience—oh my!** I used to be the kind of teenage girl who would have a fit if she was sweating, if her fingernails weren't painted or got chipped, whose hair had to be just right.

Let me tell you, that all changed once I worked for Habitat for Humanity. We mowed yards, weeded, painted houses, built porches, cleaned houses, built furniture, planted flower beds—all kinds of stuff. We slept in a gym on bleachers, and I sweated every day, but when it was all done I was so happy.

What really moved me was the elderly woman who could barely get around; we fixed up her house and yard. When we showed her the finished product, she cried. I left covered in sweat with watering eyes, poison ivy, messed-up hair, and chipped nails, but I had a heart full of joy.

Stephanie Reisor
Greenville, Texas

"We are not put on this earth for ourselves, but are placed here for each other. If you are always there for others, then in time of need, someone will be there for you."
Jeff Warner

**Volunteering has definitely made me** a more patient person. When I was younger, I would get irritated easily with someone who perhaps was too slow, or too loud, or too whatever. Now I just try to take a deep breath, realize that they may have issues I don't know about, and hear them out. This has helped me tremendously in customer service situations and in interactions with coworkers.

Karri Moss
Pinckneyville, Illinois

## Voices of Change:
## Deepak Chopra

I was on a book tour on 9/11, and I left New York on a flight to Detroit just 15 minutes before the hijacked flight left Newark airport. My son left New York (for Los Angeles) around the same time, and I was under the assumption that he had taken a United flight. By the time we landed in Detroit, the World Trade Center towers had come down. Since my son was going to L.A., and he had taken a United flight, I was sure he was on one of the hijacked flights. My wife was also on an airplane at that time, on a flight from England to New York. By the time her flight got to New York, it was forced to turn back. I didn't know where she was or where my son was. I experienced a tremendous amount of anguish. I sat in my hotel room in Detroit, watching the news on TV and crying.

I spent eight hours feeling this pain and despair until, finally, my son called. He was in Cincinnati; because he had frequent flyer miles, he had taken a different flight. He was supposed to be on that Los Angeles United flight that was hijacked. Then I heard from my wife, and she was OK too.

I felt a tremendous sense of relief and thanksgiving, and then, for the first time in my life, I realized that this is the way a lot of people must feel every day, especially in the Middle East. If you're a parent or father or husband, and you lose someone, you must feel like this. I realized that, in a way, we are so separated from the anguish of our fellow human beings. We are divorced from what is happening around the world right now. I know it now; I feel it much more in my body. I can see what others are going through, and I have a great amount of compassion for them. Compassion is the prelude to love. Without compassion, there cannot be love. And without love, there cannot be healing.

After this experience on 9/11, like many authors, I felt that the work I was promoting was not relevant anymore. So instead of continuing with my book tour, I took a car and drove west. Every day I would stop in little towns and go to a Unity church and do a prayer. And then I would do what's called a *satsangh*. It means community: people who are gathered in the name of community to discuss various things going on in the world. When I first started doing this, 10 people joined me. The second day, there were 50. By the time I got to Denver, 3,000 people showed up.

Now we do them frequently. We have an organization in New York. There is no charge for these meetings. We are calling these groups 'peace cells.' We sit and talk about whatever, and we have added other elements. After *satsangh*, we engage in *seva:* selfless service. We pick a project that we want to focus on. For instance, we recently decided to feed homeless people in Manhattan once a week by using food that local restaurants normally would throw away. And now all these restaurants are involved in feeding the homeless. And we end each peace cell with *simran,* which means remembrance; to remember who you are, to take a moment of reflection, silence, meditation.

Through the Alliance for a New Humanity (www.anhglobal. org), we are trying to connect these peace cells to each other. We have set them up in Holland, Argentina, Italy, Ireland, and England. Once we have them all over the world, we'll link them through the Internet to facilitate their collaboration with each other and discussion about projects.

My family is involved too, but sometimes we feel a little helpless. It's frustrating when people don't realize the magnitude of everything that is going on around us. Global warming right now is a crisis. In 10 years, Florida coastal areas and many other areas could disappear. And it's all connected to other things: terrorism, greed for oil, disease. They're all connected. Sometimes it feels so monumental, it's frustrating when it seems that no one else notices. So you ask yourself: What can I do? We can all do a little bit.

I don't think you do community service for anyone or anything. You do it for yourself. There's a lot of good feeling that comes from that experience. In the end, you find that whatever you put into it comes back to you tenfold.

*Deepak Chopra is an international best-selling author. His books include* The Seven Spiritual Laws of Success, Peace Is the Way, *and* How to Know God. *Since 1996, he has run the Chopra Center for Well Being in San Diego. He is the cofounder and president of the Alliance for a New Humanity.*

**Aside from affecting the course of my life** professionally, volunteering has helped me find my vocation. As the writer and preacher Frederick Buechner says, "Vocation is the place where your heart's deep gladness meets the world's deep need." I am grateful to have found my vocation: working with at-risk youth.

Hal Cato
Nashville, Tennessee

**On the six-month anniversary of 9/11,** a ceremony was held for World Trade Center victims. I volunteered to work the family check-in, in an area only the victims' family members were allowed to enter. From time to time, the grief of the whole situation was just too fresh, and some of the police officers who were working the event became overwhelmed. So I jumped in and worked the door. Here's little me, telling some foreign ambassadors, "I'm sorry, you can't come in this way." But someone had to do it, so I just did.

Sherry Lynn Fazio
New York, New York

**There is a deeper spirit that exists** in nature and connects us all. The way to tap into it is with service work. Only then can we really start to understand the positive impact we can have on others. By helping others, I also start to develop myself and my personality. I subscribe partly to the existential philosophy that we are made up of what we do and how we act in the world. By positively helping others, we are constantly positively constructing ourselves.

Pamela Cuce
Boca Raton, Florida

**You don't have to be a religious** or spiritual person to experience the beauty that comes from acts of human understanding and kindness. This rare connection has the power to cross social, cultural, and racial boundaries that have plagued our planet for centuries. By merely putting aside ego, judgments, fear, and pessimism, the smallest offering of support for a stranger can last forever within the giver and the receiver. That's how I got hooked. Give a week, then a year—you'll be "converted" for life.

Amy DeHuff
New Orleans, Louisiana

**When I was 19 I joined AmeriCorps in California,** almost by accident, really. I had been a pretty crazy teenager, without a lot of moral integrity. All of a sudden, I found myself in a mentorship position with at-risk teenagers from Oakland.

I realized that I couldn't very well counsel them to be good, conscientious people when I was still not sure where I stood in my own life. It was interesting to see all this goodness coming out of me; I didn't know exactly where it was coming from. I really turned my life around in that year, trying to make myself worthy of the advice I was giving these kids. It's how I became who I am in a lot of ways.

Besha Rodell
Chapel Hill, North Carolina

Begun in 1994, AmeriCorps provides opportunities for Americans to make an intensive commitment to service. For more information, visit www.national service.org.

# BE THE CHANGE!

## Voices of Change:
## Mark Hass

"My brother was born in a small, dusty, coal-mining town in eastern Ukraine, a decade before me and an unimaginable distance from the hospital in Brooklyn in which I came into the world. His name was Edward, but my mother called him Edik. When I was growing up, the sound of his name coming from her own lips was the only thing that ever made her cry.

Edik died before his first birthday, in that same Ukrainian town, of malnutrition and hunger, and I never knew him. Nor would I have ever imagined that his brief life would have such a lasting impact on my own. He left a legacy with me—a burden—to do what I could to ensure that no person, anywhere in the world, ever again would die of hunger.

While that goal may be unattainable, it is nonetheless the nucleus for my volunteer activities. Everyone who donates time or money to a cause has this: a reason at the core for giving of themselves to help others.

It was for Edik that, in college, I worked the food line a couple of nights each week at the Salvation Army men's shelter. For him, I have made financial donations my entire working life to food banks. He's why I have served on the board of food rescue organizations in Detroit and raised funds from reluctant friends and business colleagues for hunger relief organizations. He's why I buy bagels for homeless guys on the streets of New York.

I believe that by doing these things I can heal my small corner of the world. I believe all this makes a difference in people's lives. And I can't help imagining what would have been if someone could have made a difference in his life.

*Mark Hass is the CEO of Manning Selvage & Lee (MS&L). MS&L is a member of Hands On Network's Corporate Service Council, an alliance of more than 60 CEOs and civic leaders mobilizing the corporate workforce to serve local communities and create immediate, tangible impact in the areas of children and education, health and wellness, and the environment.*

# BE THE CHANGE!

**I have evolved my thinking** about the root of social issues because I understand more about what the people I help are going through. When I first started volunteering, I would see someone on the street and think, "Well, he's probably a drug addict." But now I understand that there are many reasons someone can go broke and become homeless.

Linda Craine
New York, New York

**When I was in ninth grade,** I joined a local school group called the Leadership Team. It was a cool group to join because your job was to assist the P.E. teachers and help with the classes. (Basically, you joined because you got to blow a whistle and be in charge of other, younger kids.)

The class I was assigned to was the special education class. It was a class of about 10 students with severe disabilities. When I first walked in, I wanted no part of trying to help students whom I could not understand, who drooled, and who wore diapers. But this was the only class that fit my schedule. When I helped a boy with Down syndrome throw a basketball, I knew I had found my life's calling. He didn't make the basket, but it didn't matter. The excitement on his face and the determination with which he threw the ball really helped me understand what life was about; it was about helping others. It was at this time I decided to become a special education teacher. I earned a master's in special education and just completed my ninth year of teaching.

Linda Mocchio
Richmond, Virginia

**Through service I have learned** that loving and being kind doesn't mean allowing myself to be manipulated. I've learned to say no when it is appropriate and to listen and pay attention to what others have to say. I've developed empathy and compassion tempered with respect for myself and others.

Patti Shepad
Keizer, Oregon

**My involvement in the community** and in politics has made me see that there really is a way around any problem. Without my political involvement, I would feel more hopeless and frustrated about all aspects of my life.

Lisa Danielson
Seattle, Washington

"What lies behind us and what lies before us are tiny matters compared to what lies within us."
Ralph Waldo Emerson

**Community service has transformed me** by creating a healthy balance in my life. Before I began volunteering, all I did was work, play soccer, and go to bars. Now I have added meaning in my life. I have a much greater understanding (and appreciation) of at-risk kids, and I think I'm a better person for it. I am also a better citizen. I now know I can make better choices politically as opposed to just getting my information from reading the newspaper or watching TV for 30 minutes.

Richard Goldsmith
Atlanta, Georgia

**Volunteering with seven- and eight-year-old kids** and helping them improve their baseball skills has helped me to understand my own son better. When you are only exposed to one seven-year-old boy each day, you wonder if the challenges and joys you experience are unique. But being with all these other kids has shown me how similar they all are in so many ways. I don't have to wonder anymore if my son's occasional temper tantrums about learning new things are unusual because I see them more than I'd like when the kids can't grasp some concept I'm trying to teach.

Rorry Hollenbeck
Jamestown, New York

To learn more about fraternities, sororities, and their philanthropic and volunteer work, log on to www.fraternity advisors.org/ Links/Fraternal_ Organizations. aspx.

**My first volunteer experience** was when I was 15, and it wasn't exactly voluntary. I had been caught shoplifting and was required to do community service. It was something I honestly had been wanting to do, but I didn't know how to get into it. I ended up spending several weekends working in a soup kitchen in a not-so-great part of town. I was scared at first, but most of the people, workers and eaters alike, were pretty nice. It made me realize that I had a pretty good life and needed to straighten up a bit.

Several years later, I helped charter a chapter of Alpha Phi Omega, the national coed service fraternity, and those were the most fulfilling times of my college career.

Jodi Bonner
Jacksonville, Florida

**A while ago, I became acquainted** with a man named Terry Karl. In my town, everyone knew him and thought him to be a very positive person. He was well known for not only his volunteer work and contributions to the community, but also for the comforting aura he always seemed to have.

At the beginning of my junior year of high school, I began to notice that Mr. Karl was looking very ill. His skin color had changed, and he looked very fragile. I was told later that day that he was dying. Not having known him very well, I was surprised when tears sprang to my eyes. A few weeks later, while on a retreat for school, a counselor asked us to talk about our feelings for Mr. Karl. I again began to cry as I spoke of what an amazing man he is and how he is known by his service to the community. I could not understand why something so horrible had to happen to him. The counselor suggested that I let Mr. Karl know how I felt.

The next day, I sat down and wrote him a letter. In the letter I told him what an inspiration he was, not only to me, but to everyone in the community, and how just by being in his presence, people were enlightened. A day or two later, I came home to see a basket of flowers with a card attached that I still read to this day and will cherish always. It was from Mr. Karl, telling of how that letter helped his healing. By writing him that letter, I was simply doing what he stood for: making a positive difference in someone else's life.

A few weeks later, I saw him at a football game and conversed with him for the first time since I received his flowers. People were lined up waiting to talk to him. Finally, we had an opportunity to talk. He gave me a tight hug and thanked me for the kind words I had written.

Not too long ago, I once again stood in line to see him. But this line was to say goodbye. Mr. Karl has not only left a lasting impression on me, but one the whole community will treasure. By putting your words into action as I did by writing that letter, you become the change.

Amber Mauriello
Sparta, New Jersey

# BE THE CHANGE!

**Volunteering has changed me in several ways.** As someone living with cerebral palsy, I no longer wait for people to do things for me. I often shock them when they see me do a task and complete it myself. Volunteering has shown me that, given a chance, it is possible for someone who is disabled to make a difference.

Additionally, volunteer work has made me less focused on and concerned about my disability. It has also taught me first aid, CPR, and many other skills that I would never have gotten involved in.

Doug Clegg
Phillipsburg, New Jersey

**I have experienced progressive loss** of my vision due to a genetic disease. Because of my condition, I was asked to give a talk to a group of third-graders. So many people think, "Oh my gosh, I have to stand in front of a group of people and give a talk." Now try to imagine doing it blindfolded. I was scared to death. I'm always afraid of being judged for many things: looks, mannerisms, you name it.

Turned out, they didn't care one bit about all that! They just knew this blind lady was coming to teach them about blind people, and they were really excited. Once I got over being so scared, it went wonderfully. They asked me questions, and I helped them understand blind people better. Now when I volunteer at that school, the kids all help me find doors and tell me when things are in my path. By helping them, they help me. I learned that I could have a large impact in my community by doing advocacy work, public education activities, and motivational speaking.

Aadria Brown
Wellington, Colorado

**My first volunteer experience was enlightening** because I had never realized how many people in my small town were homeless. I had always thought that only big cities had people sleeping out on park benches and such. Knowing this gave me an emotional push to help more people.

Celena Gibson
Bluff City, Tennessee

**When I first began volunteering** with homeless people, I was actually afraid of them. I'd been taught to stay away from people on the street and never give them money. But one day a friend and I became aware of a group of about 30 to 50 homeless people who slept in the parking lot outside a church. The autumn nights were really chilly, and I wondered if there'd be a way to bring blankets out for all the people who stayed there.

A friend and I decided to team up with a local college group, Hope for the Homeless. We told them our idea, and they helped us start a blanket collection. Altogether, we collected more than 50 blankets. When it was time to deliver them, I wanted it to be a very personal delivery, not some big, cold organizational project—just two girls who cared and wanted to bring some warmth.

We gathered a few friends together and ventured out into the cold night to deliver the blankets. I was a little nervous, a little hesitant. There was no need to be. We arrived carrying armfuls of heavy blankets, and the people smiled and thanked us. We conversed for about half an hour before we had to leave. That night, I learned not to hesitate.

Heather Leah
Raleigh, North Carolina

# BE THE CHANGE!

## Voices of Change:
## Wanda Stafford-Carter

Seventeen years ago, my daughter died, leaving behind a one-month-old and a one-year-old. Without a second thought, I took in my grandbabies, leaving me no time to mourn. With my son graduating from college the day after my daughter's funeral, and another son continuing in higher education, I continued my obligations with faith and courage.

In 1992, I lost my job of eight years. My husband thought it would be a great opportunity for me to be a stay-at-home grandma. I enjoyed being at home to greet my grandkids after school with cookies and milk, go to the school to read to a class, join the PTA, attend school programs during the day, or even get a manicure. It was amazing! After enjoying some time off, I decided to go back to work.

In September 1999, I came home from running errands to find my husband sitting on the side of the bed telling me he wanted to go to the hospital. He looked very tired and weary, so I took him to the emergency room. At the hospital, we were informed that if my husband made it through the night, it would be a miracle. He had cancer that had spread, and there was nothing they could do. Fortunately, he made it through the night.

The next day was supposed to be my first day back at work. I did not want to leave my husband's side, but I knew that I needed to go. Around 10 a.m., I received a phone call from the hospital and was told my husband had gone into a coma. Two days later, he was dead.

I went into a deep depression. I was a walking zombie. I didn't stay home much because I missed him so. His death also brought on the mourning of my daughter, which I had never been able to truly release. I had to keep on going, but this time I did not think I could make it.

My friend Yolonda encouraged me to attend a volunteer meeting with her. Though I did not want to be bothered, I finally decided to go with her, just to get out of the house. We attended an orientation for volunteers at the South Dallas Cultural Center. The moment I began to volunteer, I felt better. The depression was there, but it did not consume me as much when I was giving back.

Things have certainly changed in my life. In 2005, I was awarded the Hearts of Hope Award on Valentine's Day. In 2006, I was awarded the NBC 5 Jefferson Award and nominated for the National Freedoms Foundation at Valley Forge. In addition, I've been nominated for the Governors Award and Unsung Heroes. I am also a founding member of the Southern Poverty Law Center in Montgomery, Alabama.

It truly has been an honor and also a whirlwind. There is someone out there who is depressed right now, and I say to them, find your niche and go for it—give back. You will find the old cliché is true: If you think you are doing badly, just look around. There is always someone doing worse, and maybe you can help.

*Wanda Stafford-Carter is a volunteer dedicated to making her city a better place and helping young girls and women build self-esteem. She volunteers for numerous organizations and events, such as LIFT, the South Dallas Cultural Center, African American Read-In, Nappy Hair Affair, the Tulisoma Book Fair, Girls Inc, St. Phillips School and Academy, The Black Academy of Arts and Letters, N the Know.com, the Scholarship Fund, DFW International Community Alliance, the National Campaign for Tolerance/Wall of Tolerance, Writer's Garret, and many more.*

The South Dallas Cultural Center is a multipurpose arts facility that serves the African-American artistic community. This 18,000-square-foot facility features a 100-seat black box theater, a visual arts gallery, and studios for dance, two-dimensional arts, ceramics, printmaking, and photography. The center also has a full-service digital recording studio and an education program in digital recording technology for youth and adults. For more information, visit www.dallasculture.org.

**Since I started volunteering,** hardly anything bothers me. Things that used to bother me are nothing compared to things that plague the people I serve. Now I don't care if I have the latest PC or TV. I'm happy with my life.

Janice Myers
Tampa Bay, Florida

**I'm motivated to volunteer** because I simply like to remain useful and connected to the community. I see old friends and make new acquaintances. Unfortunately, many folks my age (78) seem to feel they have outlived their usefulness. Volunteering simply contributes to my feeling that I am a useful citizen.

Bob Humphreys
Columbia, Missouri

**Sometimes things happen** in this world that act as an equalizer. Hurricane Katrina was such an event. It put people from all walks of life at the same level for a single moment in time. Wealthy, poor, black, white—all endured hours in long lines side by side in the Mississippi heat, waiting for aid. And then the volunteers came, and we too toiled by their sides, sweating in the Mississippi heat. The common lesson in all this is that we are all the same inside, in all ways that matter.

Jaimie
Biloxi, Mississippi

**Because of my interaction with people** from all walks of life (the homeless, illegal aliens, senior citizens, and children) I have become much better at clearly communicating my purposes. I am less opinionated, and a much better listener.

Rebecca Riding
Charlotte, North Carolina

**Volunteering with different groups of people** can truly help to broaden your horizons. When I started volunteering, I was working mainly with children. This led to becoming employed with the YMCA, where I met several families who had children with disabilities. I began to realize how great the need was within my community to offer support to these families. I started a support group, Parents of Handicapped Children in Chungnam, to give parents and guardians the opportunity to support one another in their everyday lives. From listening to their stories, I became motivated to form the Citizens Alliance for a Walkable Cheonan, which acted to restore lost crossings, facilitate conveniences for the handicapped, and campaign for the right to mobility for children, the elderly, and the handicapped. I wake up every day grateful that I have been able to build relationships with the families that I met through these organizations. I am a better, more aware person because of it.

Hye Ran Yoon
Cheonan, Chungcheong Man-do, South Korea

**A few weeks ago,** I was hanging out with a five-year-old who often participates in WhyServe projects. She shared her latest idea.

"I think we should build a grocery store," she said. "OK, why?" I queried. "Well, it needs to have rooms upstairs with beds," she continued. Again I asked, "Why?" "Because there are people who don't have anyplace to live. And they don't have food. So if we build them a grocery store and bedrooms, they could come to sleep and get food when they are hungry." I thanked her for her thoughtful idea and stood in awe that, at age five, she felt empowered to dream of solutions to the needs that touched her heart. "That's a wonderful idea. We should do that," I managed. "Then we should make sure there's a doctor there too. Just in case they are sick."

Many people ask me if I think young children really "get it." My response is always, "Better than we do." By actively caring for others, this child has shaped a different view of her world and her capacity to be a part of changing it. Her view looks pretty good to me.

Megan McGamey
Atlanta, Georgia

*YES! A Journal of Positive Futures* is an award-winning quarterly magazine that invites readers to be part of a global community of change makers. Each issue focuses on a theme, offering possibilities and practical steps that can lead us all to a more positive future. Each issue also contains book reviews, special features, columns, and short "indicators." To learn more, visit www.yesmagazine.org.

# BE THE CHANGE!

**Last year I had an experience** that shed new light on what service meant to me. Quietly sitting in their south Phoenix home was an elderly couple who lived a harmonious life, despite their poor living conditions. I, along with a small group of other volunteers in the community, deprived ourselves of sleeping in late on a Saturday and put our fears aside as we battled the cockroaches that infested this couple's home. The couple sat side by side and witnessed it all.

With fair warning that the home we were about to clean was literally putrid, we did what we needed to do. Armed with face masks, gloves, and cleaning supplies, we not only banned the cockroaches from making permanent residency in their home, but we unveiled the history of this couple's life. We came across family photos, Mother's Day cards, and family heirlooms in the midst of the dirt and despair that seemingly filled their home. Uncovering their belongings, I daydreamed about the life the couple had before old age weakened them, and I got lost in their gaze as they watched us walk back and forth around their home.

It isn't the end result of our hard work that lingers on in my mind, but the words of the woman who lived there. As I walked past her, she rocked back and forth, hands in a praying position, and said, "Oh, bless you, bless you all. You can walk and do all these things. God bless you." Her gratitude made me feel like I had served.

Elisha M. Mueller
Phoenix, Arizona

**Although I'd been volunteering** with my family since I was a little girl, my passion for giving back really surfaced when I was 18 years old. My freshman sociology professor had recommended a book to me that would change my life called *And the Band Played On,* a chronicle of the AIDS epidemic in the United States. During a time when HIV and AIDS still carried a heavy public stigma, I became impassioned about serving people who were living with AIDS. I signed up to volunteer 30 hours a week that summer, every hour I could spare between shifts of waiting tables, at an Atlanta AIDS hospice.

This particular organization had a ritual of lighting a candle in the foyer whenever one of the 40 residents passed away. Upon return from a week at the beach with my family, I walked into the foyer to resume my volunteer duties to find three candles burning. I was devastated. And I realized for the first time that I hadn't been the only one giving back during my hours at the hospice. All this time, I'd been making connections, and these men had given something back to me as well.

Betsy Holland
Atlanta, Georgia

# BE THE CHANGE!

**Early in my senior year of high school,** a young lady "rolled" into my life. Angela had muscular dystrophy and spent her days in a motorized wheelchair. I had seen Angela on our local telethon for many years, so I considered it an honor to meet her when she arrived as a freshman at my high school. She and I became fast friends, and she asked if I would consider coming to MDA summer camp with her the next summer. I agreed. That was 15 summers ago.

MDA summer camp is truly a magical experience. Here, children who are "kids in wheelchairs" or "kids with braces" for 51 weeks out of the year are just "kids" for one phenomenal week. It takes a huge team of people, most of whom are volunteers, to make this annual adventure happen. Our volunteers come from so many backgrounds, but whether they arrive at camp for service hours, to care for a family member, or just because it sounded like a fun thing to do, they all leave having given their hearts and souls to their respective campers for the week. Volunteers work with their campers through dancing, swimming, horseback riding, and other activities as well as assisting them with getting dressed, eating, and bathing.

Stepping away from life as a CPA to spend a week at camp gives me my "annual dose of perspective." These kids overcome so much and do it with such optimism and enthusiasm. It truly makes the little annoyances of life seem microscopic and the small triumphs seem monumental. Through my work with MDA, I have grown as a leader, a problem solver, an advocate, and a compassionate friend.

It is often said that special people leave footprints on your heart, but I tell people that these kids have left wheelchair tire tracks all over mine.

Colleen Ernst
Houston, Texas

**Service helped me more** than those I was helping. I was going through a hard time after miscarrying, but I didn't want to be sad forever. So I decided to look outside myself and care for others. These acts of service might have been small things, but they seemed like big steps in helping me heal.

Stephanie Pflaume
Durand, Ohio

**Volunteering has changed** how I raise my kids. The interest I have in putting myself in other people's shoes is a direct result of what I do at the zoo, or at other community service projects. The concept of empathy is something not just important to me, but important for me to teach my six-year-old son.

Cam Ragen
Seattle, Washington

**It is incredible** that tens of thousands of people from all walks of life have managed to work together for one common goal: to do good. In working with all of the volunteers, organizers, and residents in the Gulf region, I have truly been served. I have gotten so much more out of this experience than I could have ever given.

Kristin Burlage,
New Orleans, Louisiana

**I had never really participated** in service work until I went into recovery for alcoholism almost 18 months ago. For me, service work has become the largest part of my life—it has to be, in order for my program of recovery to work. That is why I came to New Orleans in late November to take an active role in rebuilding this wonderful city. Whether it be helping someone else in recovery or victims of the hurricanes, or being of service to anyone else, in helping others I am able to find a spiritual serenity that keeps me sober and allows me to be the best person that I can be. Through the volunteer program that Hands On Network provides, I am able to humbly and gratefully give something back to a world that has given me so much.

Nicholas Bonsell
New Orleans, Louisiana

**Giving to a little girl** (as a Big Sister mentor) and helping to transform her life has given me inspiration to transform my own life—to stay motivated and make the right choices. I'm her role model now, so I need to make sure I'm teaching her the proper things. Do as I do, not as I say!

Kate Sheaffer
Dublin, Pennsylvania

## Voices of Change: Mara Kaplan

Often in our lives, there is a single defining moment when everything changes. My moment came when my son, Samuel, was three months old. We were in the doctor's office for a well-baby visit, and the doctor measured Samuel's head, then measured it again, and yet again. At that moment, I knew our lives would never be the same again.

It is because of Samuel and the needs of our family that I joined four other mothers to start an inclusive play space in Pittsburgh. I spent a year volunteering my time, writing grants, meeting with community members, picking out toys, and even painting walls to make our dreams a reality. On October 7, 1995, Center for Creative Play (CFCP) opened to rave reviews.

At that point, it became clear that Center for Creative Play needed a director and that I needed not just a job, but a passion. Ten years later, I am still here, and the trickle-down effect of the volunteer efforts of five caring people still amaze me. Not only do 45,000 visitors play at CFCP each year, but school-age children, college students, corporate groups, and senior citizens donate approximately 8,000 volunteer hours each year.

The trickle-down effect continues as Center for Creative Play grows beyond the Pittsburgh play space. Communities throughout the United States are beginning to recognize the overwhelming need for safe, welcoming places for all children to participate in unstructured play. Every week a new volunteer calls to ask how they can create a Center for Creative Play Environment in their town. Three groups have already completed their dreams, and several more are in the works.

It was because of my son that I helped start Center for Creative Play. It is because of Center for Creative Play that countless young volunteers have become caring, understanding teachers, that thousands of children have a place to play, and that existing play spaces are changing to better support children and families of all abilities. It is truly remarkable to see the impact one life can have on a society.

*Mara Kaplan is the CEO and a founding parent of the Center for Creative Play. She has worked with a variety of nonprofit organizations and published a variety of training manuals dealing with service learning.*

# REFLECTIONS

IMAGINE THAT YOU SET OUT TO DO SOMETHING for others, and in the process, you personally transform yourself and have one of the most fulfilling experiences of your life.

I know this experience firsthand. I have had a mentee named Giovanni for 10 years. Giovanni and I came together through a small grassroots community organization that intended to get a mentoring program started. In fact, it never got off the ground, but they did make one match—me and Giovanni, a 100 percent success rate, as far as I am concerned! Giovanni and I began having special outings together—going to the zoo, the playground, or baseball games. Gradually, I just started to incorporate her into my regular life. She came to work with me and developed a community of other mentors among my work colleagues. She came on family vacations and delighted my family with her zest and enthusiasm for all things having to do with boats and water. We fought about her spending more time writing and reading. And my husband occasionally, and secretly, allowed her to trade in homework assignments for a movie.

We nurtured Giovanni's love for cooking by having her throw adult dinner parties for our shared friends. She would read cookbooks and plan the menus, and we would decorate the house with flowers and candles. The parties were always a big hit for everyone, despite a small kitchen fire and a spatula baked into a cake. We would end the evenings with everyone offering Giovanni advice on a specific topic: What would we do over again if we were entering high school? Or what was the most important advice that we had ever received? Being friends with Giovanni created an excuse for posing the questions; sharing the answers reinforced our friendships with others.

# REFLECTIONS

Giovanni is now 16. She moved across the country a number of years ago, but we call each other, and she spends several weeks with us each summer. She now is old enough to help us look after our children, and she is a favorite babysitter and visitor. We continue to give her advice (my husband is focused on her staying away from all boys, while I focus on her keeping up her grades and planning post-high-school education). She keeps us grounded in pop culture, up-to-date on the shifting pressures of the teenage years, and alive to the world through her fresh perspective.

We have formed bonds with Giovanni's sister, mother, friends, and step-father. What a gift to have a stranger come into your life and become a part of your extended family, to see a young girl become a woman, and to have your young friend become a caretaker for your own children. I am not clear about the value of my mentoring to Giovanni, but I am so grateful for the lessons and gifts she has brought to my life.

M.N.

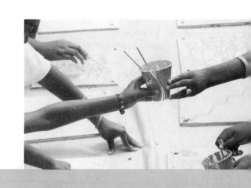

# CHAPTER 8

# Don't wait — start today
## SMALL ACTS TO CHANGE THE WORLD

S O, WHERE DO WE BEGIN? The stories and recommendations in this chapter tell us that we can begin right where we are—each and every day. Each interaction, each day shapes and affects the lives of those around us and, in turn, shapes our own lives. We affect our world with the things we decide to buy, the way that we interact with our neighbor, how much we tip our waitress. Our life is the totality of our actions, and each one adds cumulatively to the person that we are.

While perhaps hackneyed, it is nevertheless true—and even scientifically proven—that smiling affects not only the perceptions and feelings of those around us, but it also changes our own disposition. We impact the world through millions of actions over a lifetime. Each time we act, we leave an imprint, and we have the power to shape that imprint. Whether through our words, our purchasing decisions, our listening powers, our capacity to wonder and challenge the status quo, or simply our smile, we have the capacity to make a difference in the world and in ourselves.

# BE THE CHANGE!

The stories that follow remind us of the small ways that we can realize our power and the responsibility that each of us bears for all of our actions, small and large. So, read these stories and be inspired— inspired to thank a veteran, buy a cup of coffee for a police officer, drive slower, read the newspaper, or plant a flower at your local park. Even the smallest action has a ripple effect.

Read on to be challenged by some new things that you have never thought of doing, and be reminded of some things that you know you should do. Rediscover the power you hold each day to change the world and change yourself. There's no reason to wait.

**If someone says they need money** to get on the subway, I will swipe my subway pass for them and pay for their ride that way.

Allan Sih
New York, New York

**So what if your Dumpster is closer than Goodwill?** Put that stuff in your car and drive it over there. It's one of the easiest, quickest ways people can make a change.

Tamika Brown
Atlanta, Georgia

**Help the elderly who live in your community** with their household chores, or take them to doctor's appointments.

Yolanda Hilaire
Houston, Texas

**If you work in the Internet industry** and you see that a nonprofit's Web site needs work, call them up and offer to fix it for free. That's a huge help that doesn't involve you ever leaving your chair.

Joel Kunkler
Rochester, New York

**Conserve water** every single day.

John Burdett
Shoreline, Washington

Goodwill is one of the world's largest nonprofit providers of education, training, and career services for people with disadvantages, such as welfare dependency, homelessness, or lack of education or work experience, as well as those with physical, mental, and emotional disabilities. For more information, visit www.goodwill.org.

**Coach a local** youth sports team.

Luke Higginbotham
Buchanan, Virginia

**Talk to those no one else is talking to.** Allow no one to be alone.

Zaid Jilani
Kennesaw, Georgia

**Plant** a tree.

Rachel Higginbotham
Buchanan, Virginia

**When you're driving,** let someone in if they're trying to merge.

Janice Myers
Tampa Bay, Florida

**Be kind** to animals.

Melanie Mantenieks
Chicago, Illinois

**Pick up after your dog** when you go on walks.

Susan Bowman
Charlotte, North Carolina

**I'm tall, so whenever** I'm at the store and see someone who needs something off the top shelf, I get it for them.

Julia Clark
Worcester, Massachusetts


**Every day on my way to school** I bring a trash bag and pick up all the trash on the path. It keeps the environment safe, and it's a good habit to get into.

Becka MacDonald
Mission Viejo, California


**Offer directions to people** who look lost. Be an ambassador in your city. It's that simple. A few people did that for me when I first moved to New York City, and it really changed the way I viewed the city and the people who lived here.

Melissa Bieri
New York, New York


**Welcome someone new** to your neighborhood.

Mickey Paxton
Buchanan, Virginia


**Take care of the people around you,** and they'll take care of others.

Eric Silverstein
Los Angeles, California

## VOICES OF CHANGE: HARRIS WOFFORD

In 1937–38, when I was turning 12, I traveled around the world with my grandmother. That six-month trip sparked a lasting love affair with the world, and set the frame for most of my thinking about the world. I'm sure it changed my life's course.

On the eve of World War II we heard Mussolini, from his balcony, withdraw Italy from the League of Nations after the conquest of Ethiopia. Years later, I served in Addis Ababa as the Peace Corps director and special representative to Africa.

In Bethlehem on Christmas Eve, during an Arab revolt, we huddled in the Church of the Nativity while gunfire was heard in the night. In 1950, my wife and I went to Israel to work on a kibbutz and see if that form of cooperative community could be adapted by other developing nations—or in the struggling rural American South.

In Bombay, we saw Mahatma Gandhi ride through the streets. Later, stirred by Gandhi's writings, my wife and I went to India, and wrote a book together; *India Afire*. I spent much of the 1950s working in the civil rights movement to urge adoption of Gandhi's formula of civil disobedience and constructive service.

At eighteen, I enlisted in the Army Air Corps. The war ended before I could learn to fly or to fight, but from the barracks in Selma, Alabama, I wrote a book called *It's Up to Us*.

Because of my boyhood adventure, I believe in going where you have never been, and crossing national and cultural boundaries, and starting young, I now offer my six grandsons a six-week trip around the world. So far, three have made such trips, in honor of the new worlds my grandmother opened to me.

At the age of 80, I still feel like a citizen of this interdependent, warring world, which I love more than ever. And still the challenge is the one I felt in the spring of 1938: How we in the rich, predominantly white, Western world can be peacefully integrated into a surging world that is predominantly colored and poor. And "It's up to us" is still a good watchword.

**Senator Harris Wofford was the coordinator of the civil rights section of John F. Kennedy's 1960 presidential campaign. He assisted in the formation of the Peace Corps and was the CEO of the Corporation for National Service from 1995 to 2001. He was also chairman and then cochairman of America's Promise: The Alliance for Youth from 2001 to 2004.**

# BE THE CHANGE!

**My family sends daily cards** addressed to Any Sailor, thanking them for their service.

Sheri Frost
Crestview, Florida

**Plant flowers** at your park.

Jessica Marshall
New Windsor, New York

" I long to accomplish a great and noble task, but it is my chief duty to accomplish small tasks as if they were great and noble."

Helen Keller

**I'm a big fan of service starting at home.** Even if you do nothing else to serve the community, just take care of your family. Make sure you have done everything in your power to be a great parent, a great grandson. If everyone took excellent care of their family, everyone's needs would be met. Service to your family is service to others.

Danielle Boyd
Atlanta, Georgia

**Don't waste** food.

Meghan Piotrowski
Buchanan, Virginia

**Keep your dog** on a leash.

Brittany Hammock
Eagle Rock, Virginia

**Join a service-oriented civic club** or start your own. Many groups are designed to help their members make friends and make a difference, such as Kiwanis International, the Jaycees, or the Lions Club, to name a few.

Amber Smith
Raleigh, North Carolina

**Listen. Take time to get to know** the people around you. How many people do you *really* know? We pass through so many people without reaching into their soul. There is a lot of depth to this world and its people. If we only graze the surface, no greater good will ever come. The world would need less therapy if we would listen a little better and actually care.

Kim Wolfinger
Columbus, Ohio

There are almost 1.35 million Lions members in 199 countries and geographic areas. Lions Clubs work to solve challenges such as blindness, drug abuse prevention, and diabetes awareness. To learn more, log on to www.lions clubs.org.

**Learn the first names of your acquaintances**—neighbors, shop owners, servers, people who work for the same company as you but whom you don't interact with much—and greet them with their name as often as possible.

Brad Kane
Sandusky, Ohio

## How Pocket Change for Some Can Save Lives and Change the World

3¢ can supply a dose of vitamin A to boost a child's immune system and prevent blindness.

5¢ can provide enough iodized salt to prevent stunted physical and mental growth in a child for one year.

30¢ provides lifesaving antibiotics for a child suffering from pneumonia.

$1 can immunize a child against polio for life, protecting him or her against the disease and preventing its spread to nearby communities.

$2 can buy a nutritional kit for a severely malnourished child. The kit includes basic food supplements that will tide the child over until appropriate food aid can be supplied.

$3.75 can provide educational materials for a child for one year, including a portion of the cost of teacher supplies. Materials include books, pencils, a school bag, a slate board, chalk, posters, rulers, safety scissors, and notebooks.

$10 provides enough high-protein biscuits to feed three hungry children for one month.

$17 can provide a child with all the vaccinations required to provide him or her against the six major childhood diseases.

$20 can buy purification tablets to clean 104 gallons of water that would otherwise cause disease.

$60 will immunize 60 children from measles for life.

$150 pays for a small well to provide clean water for an entire village.

$250 can provide a tent for a family whose home has been destroyed during a disaster, such as an earthquake or a civil war.

# BE THE CHANGE!

**It doesn't take much time** or money to sponsor a child. I have a sponsor child in the Philippines.

Diana Hill
Bethesda, Maryland

Kiwanis International is an organization of service- and community-minded individuals who support children and young adults around the world. More than 600,000 Kiwanis family members in 96 countries respond to the needs of their communities and pool their resources to address worldwide issues. To learn more, log on to www.kiwanis.org.

**I offer my seat to elderly** passengers or pregnant women.

Carol Heinlein
Boston, Massachusetts

**I got in the habit of paying** the toll of the person behind me. Every time I would go over a certain bridge, I would pay the person's toll. It's fun to look at their reactions in the rearview mirror!

Liv Faris
Seattle, Washington

**If you don't have time or money to volunteer,** there are little things you can do to improve our world. I have one that is a personal pet peeve: If something falls off the shelf at the grocery store, pick it up! Clean up after yourself! It doesn't take that long, and if you don't do it, someone else has to.

Beth Senko
New York, New York

**Breaking the rules isn't always a bad thing.** While I was answering phones at a shelter for homeless women and children, a woman called at the end of the month, out of food and money. This was not unusual.

What *was* unusual was that there were children crying in the background. My instincts told me that these children were quite hungry and miserable. I obtained the caller's location, went to my supervisor, and advised her that I was about to break the rules. I went to a grocery store, purchased a couple of bags of food, delivered them, and went back to answering the phones.

> "We make a living by what we get, we make a life by what we give."
> Winston Churchill

M. Orozco
Fair Oaks, California

**Drive slower! You not only spare your own life,** you can also spare the lives of many small creatures that you wouldn't otherwise have time to see and avoid.

Lilli Edelsbrunner
Graz, Austria

**Cover your mouth** when you sneeze.

Todd Cline
Lawrenceville, Georgia

# BE THE CHANGE!

**Ask if your workplace has a company** matching program for employee donations to nonprofit companies. People can also look into whether their company donates to organizations that their employees are committed to.

Kerrin Grace
Boston, Massachusetts

As the largest volunteer child advocacy association in the nation, National Parent Teacher Association reminds our country of its obligations to children and provides parents and families with a powerful voice to speak on behalf of every child while providing the best tools for parents to help their children be successful students. To learn more, visit www.pta.org.

**Bring candy into work and leave it** in a dish on your desk. It invites people to stop by and gives you an opportunity to spread your contagious smile.

Dawn Hampton
Willingboro, New Jersey

**Recycle everything possible,** buy and eat organic food as much as possible, use nontoxic dish and clothing detergent, use environment-friendly products on your lawn, don't use toxic cleaners, use cloth napkins, conserve energy, use stale water for plants, open blinds to warm the house, reuse paper at work, refill bottles, give away books, magazines, and other items, donate all unused items, drive a small-engine car, and take your own bag to the market.

Stefanie Hisler
Tampa, Florida

**Tip a little extra** when you go out.

Shannon Chettle
San Francisco, California

**Get smart about issues in your community.** Read the editorial section and the letters section and see what is important to your neighbors. Is the city hosting an open forum at a library about the new highway that might end up in your neighborhood? Attend that meeting. They're dying for people to show up and it won't cost a thing.

Lisa Danielson
Seattle Washington

**The other day I was on the subway** and it was freezing. I saw this young woman wearing just long underwear and a sundress, carrying a knapsack that probably had everything she owns in it. She was pregnant and wearing a sign written in Spanish. No one spoke to her or really looked at her. It broke my heart. So I gave her a card with contact information for a nearby shelter. I always keep them on me when I go out, for cases like this.

Anne Corry
New York, New York

**Give a child a book.** If I had all the money in the world, I'd buy every kid a book. Reading gives them imagination, focus, a sense of quiet, plus reading skills that will help them all their life.

Sue Franzen
Tampa Bay, Florida

**First Book is a national non-profit organization founded in 1992 with a single mission: to give children from low-income families the opportunity to read and own their first new books. They provide an ongoing supply of new books to children in community-based mentoring, tutoring, and family literacy programs. To learn more, or to make a donation, log on to www.first book.org.**

## Voices of Change:
## Nadirah Sabír

"

I am a ninth-generation American and second-generation Muslim American. Although my immediate family is Muslim, my extended family is not, so I learned early that everyone wasn't just like me—at least not on the surface. Some spoke patois. Some fished, others farmed. Others ran businesses in the community. Some took Sabbath on Sundays, others Saturdays. What we had in common was love, respect, and goals for our family and community. There were plenty of disputes—like when a grandmother fed chicken to her vegetarian grandchild. But overall, our diversity was a source of strength in our family.

Growing up, I had exposure to Eastern and Western ways, but I was raised in an environment sheltered from the effects of classism, racism, and hypersexualized images of women. You see, growing up, I didn't feel 'different' or 'minority' or 'other.' I did not feel less worthy. That was a construct others attempted to foist on me later.

I attended a private Islamic grade school, then a public non-Muslim school, and then I worked in corporate America. Those transitions had their difficulties. My parents were not aware of the huge cultural challenges that awaited me every step of the way. They didn't understand how unsettling and

estranging it would be to go from an Islamic school environment of total acceptance to a public school that was secular
and accepting only on the surface. It gave me a taste of what
immigrants experience and what my parents had thought
they conquered in the 1960s. The response was 'Well, it's
not as bad as it used to be.'

Within the Muslim community, many think that racism,
drugs, and violence don't really touch our community. But
recently, these problems have started popping up, and many
parents have no clue how to effectively address these challenges. That's changing. Muslims are losing that sense of
'untouchableness.' They are reaching out to adults who were
raised as Muslims in America to better prepare the third and
fourth generations to navigate any environment, here or
abroad, and still maintain their identity.

While still working as an online editor at a local newspaper,
I created a lecture series for seniors at the W. D. Mohammed
High School. We touched on everyday skills—budgeting
and negotiating, teacher-student dynamics, proactive financial
aid, dealing with roommates, multiculturalism, interfaith
relations, the importance of social networks, majority-minority
dynamics today—all the conversations I wish I'd had with
someone closer to my age before heading off to college. At
the end of that senior lecture series, a few days before graduation, I issued a challenge: 'Come back to the school in five

years and invest your time in the next generation. Teach them what you've learned so far.' I knew that by then, those students will have struggled with distractions and balance and their integrity. Since then, many have told me they appreciated my sharing real-world experiences to help them bridge things to come.

*Nadirah Sabír is an award-winning multimedia journalist with experience as a writer, editor, producer, and columnist in print and online media. Her work has appeared in* Black Enterprise, Money, *and* Azizah *magazines,* The Atlanta Journal-Constitution, *and ajc.com. Her compilation of columns garnered an Atlanta Association of Black Journalists (AABJ) award in 2004. The previous year, she won honors for her poignant feature "Journey from Ground Zero," an intimate profile of three Muslim Americans involved in the emergency efforts in New York during 9/11. She also received a prize for her six-part series titled "State of Muslims in America," which received a nod in 2002 from the Council on American Islamic Relations.*

**Donate** blood.

Kenneth Coon
Tooele, Utah

**Shake hands with and thank any veteran,** of any war, that you happen to meet.

Corey Clark
Suwannee, Georgia

**If I see a turtle slowly crossing the road,** I always pull over and help it across before it gets hit.

Will Hammock
Buford, Georgia

**I'm a member of Amnesty International.** They have a freedom writer's component, where all you have to do is write a quick letter to someone about a political prisoner. So simple, so easy, and yet how meaningful and important it is for the prisoner to know they are not forgotten. It takes me less than five minutes to write a letter (Amnesty International even gives you a template), and yet, I know that letter is worth its weight in gold to someone who has given up hope that anyone even knows about them.

Dr. Rachel McClement
Glendale, California

**Amnesty International is a worldwide movement of people who campaign for internationally recognized human rights. For more information, visit www.amnesty.org.**

# BE THE CHANGE!

The Freecycle
Network is a
grassroots move-
ment of people
who are giving
(and getting)
stuff for free in
their own towns.
To learn more,
visit www.free
cycle.org.

**I am a member of a Freecycle community,** where you can post things you want and things you have to give away. It's a great way to acquire things for free and give new homes to your unwanted possessions.

Amy Woidtke
Seattle, Washington

**Just giving a person a compliment** can make their overall attitude change. This, in turn, might even make them treat others better.

Ann Munson
Pequot Lakes, Minnesota

**Carry an extra dollar in your pocket** in case you meet someone in need.

Rebecca Ridin
Charlotte, North Carolina

**If someone is short of cash** in your grocery line, give that person some money.

Elizabeth Fitzgerald
Austin, Texas

**Host a neighborhood picnic** where people can get to know each other.

Bryant Hampton
Willingboro, New Jersey

**If I see a couple or family** who look like they could use a break, sometimes I will pay for their gas at the station or their meal at a restaurant—anonymously. I like that it's anonymous, and I bet it keeps them thinking longer about kindness toward others.

Susan Kent
West Palm Beach, Florida

**Adopt a dog, don't buy** one from a pet store.

**If you have a few extra cans of food,** drop them off in a food donation bin.

**If you see someone with a petition,** listen to them and look at their brochure.

**Attend a community meeting** to find out what is happening in your neighborhood.

Jen Alltop
Bay Area, California

> Millions of young, healthy animals are euthanized each year because there are too many pets and not enough loving homes or people interested in providing food, water, shelter, and medical care to these animals. To learn more, or to find a pet shelter near you, log on to www.adopta pet.com.

**One small act I perform every day** is to bring the newspaper up to my neighbor's porch on the way home from school. She is elderly, and it is sometimes hard for her to walk all the way down her driveway to get it. I also bring down her trash cans on trash day and bring her mail to her. I know it's not much, but it's totally worth when she tells me I am "as sweet as a flower on the first day of spring."

Kiara Bynum
Glen Allen, Pennsylvania

## Voices of Change: Jill Morehouse Lum

"

Addy Walker is a doll—a character in the American Girl series, that is—who escapes from slavery with her mother in 1864. In January 2006, my six-year-old and I began dreaming of an Addy paper-doll-making and birthday party for Martin Luther King Jr. Day. But sadly, I knew we couldn't gather a diverse group on our own.

So my daughter's invitation went like this: 'If you are a white girl, bring someone who is not white. If you are a black girl, bring someone who is not black, and so on. And you have to bring a friend with you if you come.'

Some invitees' mothers sent regrets: there was not a single girl their daughter's age to call. A few other moms had a school friend in mind, but worried that her parents would bristle at the idea of such a staged party, where a child might be invited just because she fits a profile. When I called the mother of my daughter's African-American classmate, I was nervous too. Our children enjoyed each other, but she had never been to our house for a playdate. I had only passed the mom once or twice in the school halls. Was it all a little too cute? Not at all. She just said, 'Sure! Sounds like a good idea!'

In all, 25 girls and 10 moms came to our house. My husband baked his signature almond-infused birthday cake in honor of

Dr. King. We made paper dolls. We went to the playground. We sat in a circle and imagined what it would be like to do the right thing, the hard thing, in our time.

It felt risky to offer such an invitation. And as the moms met and spoke to each other, some confessed that it also felt a bit risky to respond—to go to the home of a family you have not met, or of a race that you are not, or in a part of town that is less familiar.

The party was supposed to go from 2:30 to 4. At 5:30, several of us adults were still gathered around the kitchen table.

We did not solve the problems of the world. But if little black girls and little white girls, and little white boys and little black boys, can play together, we just might.

There can be no justice without connection. Connection is little black girls, little white girls, just little girls all over the world over taking the risk of inviting a new friend to the table and, with their mothers, joining hands.

*Jill is a former schoolteacher who is passionate about learning through service and experience. She recently completed her master's degree in theology and will be ordained in the Presbyterian church.*

**Return a scowl** with a smile.

William Hylton
Raleigh, North Carolina

**My environmental science teacher,** Professor Grembowitz, was a big inspiration for me. He taught the most eye-opening and insightful class about the harm we are doing to our planet. After you hear the statistics, it's hard to look at a foam cup the same way again. Now I use cloth towels instead of paper towels to help reduce the destruction of the rain forest, I don't let my car idle and help kill the ozone, and I generally treat the environment with more respect.

Jessica DeGutis
Toms River, New Jersey

**Have a community yard sale** and give proceeds to a charity.

Rich Simpson
Philadelphia, Pennsylvania

**I write to my representatives** to tell them how I feel about their legislation. I advise others to do the same. Don't be afraid to tell them how you really feel; it's their job to represent you.

Carolyn Goodell
Granite Bay, California

**Recognize the good—and difficult**—work of police officers and fire-fighters. They have stressful jobs and are often underpaid. If you see a police officer or fire department personnel member, go up and give a kind word, or perhaps offer them a small token of your appreciation, such as a hot cup of coffee. It's unbelievable how low morale can affect a person working in those fields.

Amber Smith
Raleigh, North Carolina

**Look past uniforms and let people**—the guy who's repairing something in your home, or the woman who's emptying your office's wastebaskets—know that you see them as human beings. Thank them for their work. Look them in the eye. It makes people feel less like wallpaper.

Brenda Tran
Atlanta, Georgia

**Help with a stranger's** flat tire.

Arielle Kass
Lawrenceville, Georgia

"We should all be concerned about the future, because we have to spend the rest of our lives there."

C.f. Ketterling

**I try to write positive letters** when I receive good service in the community. If someone in the local hardware store is friendly or gives me good service, I want them and their managers to know about it. Today, so many people call companies with complaints. I like to think that I can make someone's day by telling them how they have affected me in a positive way.

Linda Mocchio
Richmond, Virginia

**I have a canvas bag in my car** filled with packs of crackers, breakfast bars, and such. When I see folks who are in need at intersections, I offer them these little food packs, as well as eye contact, a smile, and a kind word. Almost 100 percent of the time, their faces light up, they eagerly take the food that's offered, and they thank me most earnestly—usually offering a blessing for me.

Billie Pendleton-Parker
Atlanta, Georgia

**Get involved** in your Community Watch program.

Jonathan Weaver
Raleigh, North Carolina

**My grandfather posted** a note on each of his phones. It said simply, "Remember the feathers." Seeing this phrase would remind him of an old Jewish fable:

A man asks a rabbi what he can do to gain the forgiveness of a friend about whom he had spoken badly to others. The rabbi instructs the man to climb to the top of a hill and break open a pillow, letting the feathers scatter in the wind. He is then instructed to return a day later and collect all the feathers. "Impossible," the man says to the rabbi.

The rabbi answered, "So it is with the words we speak; it is impossible to collect them all, regardless of how desperately we try."

I remember the feathers; I try to speak kindly of others.

Beth Reingold Gluck
Atlanta, Georgia

"We must not, in trying to think about how we can make a big difference, ignore the small daily differences we can make which, over time, add up to big differences that we often cannot foresee."

Marian Wright Edelman

267

## Voices of Change:
## Tamika Catchings

"

From the time I was a little girl, I've set goals and dreamed big. I was blessed with parents who pushed me to be the very best and taught me the importance of giving back and making a difference in as many lives as I could.

Growing up, I was always around my father, Harvey, an 11-year NBA veteran. My brother, sister, mother, and I attended numerous community service events with him and his teammates. I remember telling myself as a child that if I ever got the chance to give back and to make a difference in others' lives, I would. As a young girl, I made it my life's purpose to encourage as many people as possible, especially kids.

The opportunity to reach out to others presented itself in college, when I began playing basketball for the Tennessee Lady Volunteers. Coach Pat Summitt ingrained in each member of the team the importance of using your talents and taking the time to make a difference in the lives of others.

The real transformation started when I finished college and began making my own choices. My dream of encouraging young people became a reality when I hosted my first Catch the Fever basketball camp, which taught young girls and boys basketball fundamentals as well as the importance of sports-

manship. After growing the camp and adding more programs, I founded the Catch the Stars Foundation in 2004.

I'm very proud to have accomplished many things on the
basketball court, in the classroom, and in life. Howerver,
among my proudest achievements are the many lives that
I've been fortunate to touch and the encouragement I've
been able to share with people from different walks of life.
Bringing smiles to faces, motivating, and mentoring are little
things that make big differences and give me more satisfaction than any amount of money or experience ever could.

Each of us, whether famous or not, has the ability to make
an impact on someone's life by doing something as simple as
grabbing a hand, giving a compliment, or even exchanging a
smile. You never know how the smallest gesture or a new
relationship can change a life, including your own.

I enjoy watching kids that I've mentored and guided blossom into young women and men and then reach back to
guide others in the right direction. It's also a blessing to keep
in touch with adults and mentors who have helped me during my life. Many of them continue to share knowledge,
support, and encouragement, and I'm lucky to have so many
positive people in my life.

When my basketball career ends, I'll continue to be the same
positive person, and I'll continue building relationships in
the community. The Catch the Stars Foundation will still be

around to mentor and encourage youth to be all that they can be.

I don't wish to be remembered for the number of points I scored as a Lady Vol, WNBA player, or Olympian. I also don't wish to be remembered for the number of degrees or the amount of money I earned, but instead for the number of lives I touched.

Building relationships in the community fills my heart and helps me to continue to blossom into a person that my parents and God would be proud of.

*Tamika Catchings was awarded the WNBA Rookie of the Year award in 2002. She was the runner-up for the league's MVP and Defensive Player of the Year, and she became the first Indiana Fever player ever to be named to the All-WNBA First Team. Following the 2002 WNBA season, she helped lead the United States National Team to a gold medal in the 2002 FIBA World Basketball Championship for Women.*

WE ALL UNDERESTIMATE OUR POWER to make a difference. We lose sight of our ability to improve the worlds of our neighbors and friends with small gestures of kindness. We fail to recognize how our unique gifts and passion can affect our communities and neighborhoods.

Sometimes by doing something to delight ourselves, we make a difference for others. My friend Daphne has traveled the world in her lifetime—motorcycling through Soviet Russia, piloting planes over Mexico, and living a life of seeking and learning. When she moved into a small house in a neighborhood with a reputation for crime and drugs, her friends and family expressed concern. Despite several small burglaries and a purse snatching, Daphne was undaunted. She made friends with other seniors and entertained the children of the neighborhood with small tokens from her travels that to them were treasures. Daphne also started to work each day to create a garden in the vacant lot next to her house, transforming it into sections that included a maze of stones brought in from around the neighborhood, a Japanese meditation station complete with a lily pool, a profusion of brightly colored flowers, and a miraculous fountain centerpiece. Neighborhood children watched at first, then joined in the garden's construction. Bus drivers and motorists honked in delight as they drove by. The garden, constructed on a piece of land abandoned by the city, had no official purpose, no long-term intent, but its spirit of whimsy brought people together in a communion of shared delight.

May we all tend our own life's gardens with generosity of spirit and joy.

M.N.

# CHAPTER 9

# The gift that keeps giving

## INSPIRING MOMENTS IN SERVICE

W E END WITH A SET OF STORIES THAT REMIND us how serving others is truly a gift. Service is a gift of ourselves that we give to the world, for which, in return, we receive bountiful and unexpected gifts of our own. The stories throughout this book have related how acts of service have profoundly affected the lives of those serving as well as those served. Service offers transformational encounters, just singing for and getting to know the residents of a nursing home or seeing how the gift of a single coat can entirely change a life. Often, the experiences of service are ones that stay with us for a lifetime. They become reminders that we carry with us of our own blessings, of the need for compassion, and especially, of our own power to effect change.

Robert F. Kennedy said, "Each time a person stands up for an ideal, or acts to improve the lot of others … he sends forth a tiny ripple of hope, and crossing each other from a million different centers of energy and daring, those ripples build a current that can sweep down the mightiest walls of oppression and resistance."

# BE THE CHANGE!

Each one of us has the potential to change our world, and the stories in this chapter will nourish and cultivate the seeds of change that are growing within you. A single moment can be the catalyst for a lifetime commitment to service. The unexpected generosity of a homeless man or the grateful smile of a six-year-old may be enough to change your life—and enough to inspire you to change the lives of others. Change ripples out and then waves back over us—cleaning, rejuvenating, and restoring.

**Mr. Parker lived in a small one-room apartment** at a local retirement home, where he had been moved after his first room had caught fire. The staff had moved all of his belongings, but they had never cleaned the soot and ash off them, and they just kind of put stuff wherever it landed. Mr. Parker was in a wheelchair and couldn't walk around and straighten or clean things.

One day a friend and I went to help him. We spent six hours cleaning a room the size of a walk-in closet. We threw out trash, found old family pictures, and framed them for him. It looked great. He cried when we left and made a comment I will never forget: "It's too bad that I had to get cancer to meet such nice people."

Melissa Chaney
Columbus, Georgia

"Remember that when you leave this earth, you can take with you nothing that you have received—only what you have given: a full heart, enriched by honest service, love, sacrifice, and courage."
St. Francis of Assisi

**I once volunteered at a Christmas** event where they gave out candy canes and a coat to everyone who came in off the street. One of the other volunteers was coughing really hard, and a homeless client walked up to her, split his candy cane in half, and gave it to her, saying, "You sound like you can really use this." Forget what the volunteers were doing there; *that* was a scene of true generosity.

Anne Corry
New York, New York

## Voices of Change:
## David Bornstein

"

I first learned about social entrepreneurs in the early 1990s, while I was researching a book on Grameen Bank. I had been working as a newspaper reporter in New York City for a few years when I read an article about a 'village bank' in Bangladesh that made loans only to poor villagers, and almost exclusively to women. At the time, Grameen Bank had a half a million borrowers, who were able to advance themselves slowly out of hard-core poverty through self-employment. The bank had been referred to as a development 'miracle.'

It seemed unbelievable; I couldn't shake the story from my mind. Most of the news stories I had written did nothing to alter my view of the world, but the story of Grameen Bank challenged my perceptions. Was it really possible to overcome such entrenched poverty? I decided to go to Bangladesh to see it for myself. For six months, I saved money to make the trip.

On the flight there, I thought that I was probably wasting my time. But a week after landing, I found myself in a village, sitting cross-legged on a bamboo mat, interviewing villagers—primarily the women who received the loans—about their lives. I spent months talking to people this way. It was a transformative experience. I began to see how so many of my own assumptions about 'the poor' were profoundly misguided.

The women were funny, savvy, competent, and surprisingly forthcoming. They explained that with their loans, $70 a year on average, they would purchase something like a cow or a sewing machine, and with the income they earned, they would pay off the loan in weekly installments. At the end of the year, they would own the cow or the sewing machine. Most of them had never before owned any significant productive assets. Many described how over time, they were able to move from very oppressive poverty (eating one or two meals a day) to less oppressive poverty (eating three meals a day, keeping a vegetable garden, having a tin roof, and being able to send their children, including their daughters, to school).

When I first began investigating Grameen Bank, I was surprised to discover that it had been initiated by one person, a Bangladeshi economist named Muhammad Yunus. I saw that Yunus was probably the most successful entrepreneur I had ever met, except that he was cut from a different cloth. He wasn't interested in getting rich; his dream was to 'put poverty in the museum.'

My experiences in Bangladesh gave me great hope. I learned that it was possible to solve problems that I had once thought were intractable. I also realized that a powerful way to produce more innovative solutions, like Grameen Bank's, would be to find and support the people who devote their lives to building them, like Muhammad Yunus.

Shortly after my trip to Bangladesh, I met a man named Bill Drayton, an American who had founded a remarkable organization called Ashoka: Innovators for the Public, which searches the globe to find and support social entrepreneurs. Ashoka has supported more than 1,600 innovators in more than 50 countries, providing them with financing and connecting them in a fellowship so they can collaborate, exchange ideas, and carve out a new profession. When I heard about Ashoka, I was captivated by the idea of a global fellowship of ethical change makers, and I wondered: What were they all doing?

I spent five years traveling to eight countries and interviewing more than 100 social entrepreneurs. And I came away from the experience with a view of the world that was stunningly different from the picture I got from the news media. Rather than a world filled with terrorists and celebrities and political hucksters, I got a glimpse of a new sector emerging, populated by people like Muhammad Yunus. I found that these entrepreneurs were struggling with and in many cases succeeding against high odds—protecting street children across India, safeguarding the environment in Brazil, building more effective schools in the United States, increasing access to health care in South Africa, reforming the legal system in Poland, creating independent living centers for disabled people in Hungary, and more.

Most Americans know almost nothing about these people. We need to ask why we hear so much about our social ills, but not our cures. What would happen if we could see society through a new lens—a lens of social innovation? If we could see the potential and opportunity, the full range of activity that is occurring across society today, would we become less fearful and more hopeful about the future? If the work of the social entrepreneurs demonstrates one thing above all, it is that people who change the world have to believe that change is possible. This belief does not arrive magically. People need to hear and see what others are doing. They need stories to build their courage and faith. Most important, they need to see that those who change the world always begin humbly. You don't have to possess the knowledge or the skill or the energy to complete a task when you begin it; you just need enough to begin. More will come.

*David Bornstein is a journalist who specializes in writing about social innovation. He has authored two books:* The Price of a Dream: The Story of the Grameen Bank *and* How to Change the World: Social Entrepreneurs and the Power of New Ideas.

Ashoka identifies and invests in leading social entrepreneurs—extraordinary individuals with unprecedented ideas for change in their communities—supporting them, their ideas, and their institutions through all phases of their careers. Ashoka has invested in more than 1,700 Ashoka Fellows in 60 countries. To learn more about Ashoka, log on to www.ashoka.org.

# BE THE CHANGE!

**I had a quarter-life crisis** when I was 23. Like many people during the dot-com boom in 1999, I found myself working till 2 a.m., six days a week. It was fun at first—working hard, playing hard—but for some reason, I felt that there was something missing. I took a long look at what I was doing with my time and realized that up until that point, I had not been volunteering and doing things that benefited others in the community and made me feel good about myself. My peers were in the same situation.

Having volunteered for several pediatric AIDS organizations while in school, I knew that the simple and inexpensive needs of children living with the disease were not being met. I decided to match the needs of the children with the resources of business professionals.

I took a week off work and decided that I would help myself and my friends by inventing the concept of digital philanthropy through Angelwish.org, where we post the wishes of children living with HIV/AIDS all over the world and make it simple for a busy person to grant the wish. Putting the giving process online made it convenient for everyone to use. By personalizing the Web site with the names, ages, and wishes of several thousand children living with HIV/AIDS, we made it more than the typical "charity by check." Donors select where and to whom they want to give online and know that 100 percent of their contribution is going to the recipient.

In the seven years since I created it, Angelwish has grown to become an international organization supporting more than 125 HIV/AIDS care centers in 15 countries. Knowing that I played a part is truly rewarding.

Shimmy Mehta
Jersey City, New Jersey

**My husband and I are musicians.** Once we were hosting a Christmas party with some other musicians and decided it would be nice to go caroling at a nearby nursing home. We certainly were surprised to learn that at that time of year, the nursing home had people coming to visit and entertain every hour of every day, and we actually had to sign up for a time slot.

We signed up and the people really liked us, but we felt really sad when we were leaving because we realized that these folks had so many people coming around Christmastime—I mean, they must get sick of it—but come January or February, there'd be nobody.

> "forget yourself for others and others will never forget you."
>
> Unknown

So we decided to make plans to go there once a month to perform. We called ourselves "La Compagnie" because "Viva La Compagnie" was a really popular song with them. It was great—we'd do mostly show tunes, and then we'd try to include seasonal numbers, like love songs for Valentine's Day or Irish tunes in March. When we were finished, people would always come up to us and make requests for the next performance, and we'd always try to learn those songs.

But the best part of the experience was this: After we introduced ourselves, we'd go around and have them introduce themselves and talk about where they had come from and what they had done in their lives. They just loved that part, and we realized they didn't get to talk about themselves very often. It was fascinating and humbling to learn about each person. So singing was really only half of the experience—the other half, and the best part, was just getting to meet and talk to these interesting people.

Kami Lyle
Harwich, Massachusetts

# BE THE CHANGE!

**I work with a group** of developmentally disabled adults. Every month, a group of volunteers goes to group homes and takes the residents bowling, or we stay in and work on scrapbooks and have pizza parties. One of the older residents, a guy in his early 50s named Wes, once said to me, "Bob, let me tell you something. I think you're a good man." I could live off that compliment for the next 10 years.

Bob Young
Charlotte, North Carolina

**Volunteering can really highlight** the best and worst in humanity. The first AIDS patient I ever was assigned to help was named John. He was in his 40s and so completely wasted by the disease I didn't recognize him in the photos in his apartment until he pointed them out.

AIDS Action is a national organization dedicated to the development, analysis, cultivation, and encouragement of sound policies and programs in response to the HIV epidemic. For more information, visit www.aids action.org.

One of my tasks was to get him downstairs and into a cab to get to his doctor. One reason I was there, besides physically helping him walk, was to see that cabs would stop for him. He would try to flag down a cab alone, and they would see this poor suffering man and drive away. It was horrible.

But John more than made up for it. The amount of bravery it took him to get through the day was inspiring. He just kept on, navigating the medical system, filling out endless forms, and just plain getting up and getting through his day. He had more gumption than most healthy people I've ever met.

Gary Bagley
New York, New York

**I first met Daquan when** he was in second grade. After getting to know him through a local after-school program, I was flattered when he asked me to have lunch with him at his school. I did and ended up talking with his teacher about his performance in the classroom. Although the teacher indicated that Daquan was very smart, she said he was behind his grade level in reading and she was worried about his transition the following year to elementary school. Trying to encourage Daquan in his reading, I bought him four Learn to Read books to read over the summer; at my request, he would call me each week to check in and let me know how his reading was going. I continued to work with Daquan the following year, stopping by his school to see him and continuing to meet with his teachers to talk about his academic progress. Imagine my joy and surprise when, at the end of his third-grade year, Daquan invited me to his school's awards assembly, where he received an award for reading the most books of any child in school during the school year! My work with Daquan, who is one of eight children in an impoverished family, has shown this great kid that someone besides his mother cares and believes in him; it has also allowed him to begin dreaming about going to college and to know that he will have the support needed to succeed. My time spent with Daquan has meant, for me, a chance to make a difference in the life of an intelligent and dynamic kid and to feel good knowing that he now sees the limitless possibilities his future holds.

Laura McCrodden
Atlanta, Georgia

> "What we do for ourselves dies with us. What we do for others and the world remains and is immortal."
> Albert Pine

283

**When you can actually see the change** that you have made in someone's life firsthand, it's brilliant. I was once volunteering at a local elementary school, and in the process I met a little boy. He put on a brave face every day as he came to school—you would never know that his mom's cancer treatments were failing.

When I found out about his troubles at home, I wanted to do something special for him. I decided that I could be his secret pal—leave him inspirational notes or small gifts to cheer him up. One day I saw him finding the crayons and a coloring book I had gotten for him, and he was grinning from ear to ear. Maybe I made him feel better even if it was just for a second. All the inspiration I need was that big, pearly white smile.

Rebekah Lightfoot
Waldo, Arkansas

**I grew up in an area** where many Vietnamese families had settled after coming from Vietnam in the late 1970s. I recall one girl who entered our sixth-grade class midyear, not knowing a word of English. She would sit by herself at lunch, at recess, and in class. I invited her to play hopscotch, which she learned quickly. I ended up becoming her tutor, starting out by sounding out words with her. At that time, it didn't seem like I did anything special. After the school year ended, we did not keep in touch, and we went our separate ways to different middle and high schools.

In my last year of college, I took an English class, and on the first day we went around the room introducing ourselves. After class, someone tapped me on the shoulder and explained who she was—it was the Vietnamese girl I had tutored a decade ago, who told me how nice I had been to her. I will never forget it!

Denise Louie
San Francisco, California

**While growing up in a small town** in northern Utah, I received many opportunities for personal growth and development through participation in community, school, and church activities. One program that greatly influenced my life was the Boy Scouts of America. Through dedicated volunteer scoutmasters and other leaders who oversaw our scout troop activities, we took memorable camping, backpacking, and hiking trips, attended scout camp each summer, and learned important skills like swimming, lifesaving, first aid, and outdoor survival. Equally important, we had opportunities to learn leadership, citizenship, and life skills by serving in leadership positions within our own troop and being involved in our community.

The numerous positive experiences I had as a Boy Scout more than 20 years ago still motivate me to give back to the program that provided me so many great memories and opportunities for growth. Wherever I have lived, I have found opportunities to volunteer as an adult leader with local troops. In volunteering, I have worked to achieve the Boy Scouts of America's organizational goal of helping boys develop into honorable men through meaningful activities. Currently, I volunteer as a scoutmaster in Sugar Land, Texas, where I share my experiences with the current generation of scouts, which includes my own 12-year-old son.

Carl Hulet
Houston, Texas

**I began work at Center City Churches'** MANNA food pantry four years ago, during my seventh year of retirement. I had served on church committees in the past, but I had never been "in the trenches," meeting people who are in need face-to-face. I had to remedy this deficiency. To prepare myself for service at the pantry, I took a "sabbatical" from retirement and went to school to improve my Spanish language skills.

The vast majority of people I meet at the pantry are beautiful in spirit and soul: caring, humble, and unselfish people who, through no fault of their own, are caught in a life that demands resources they lack. These people are my friends, and I regard my work with them as sharing, not giving. Initially, I wondered how a couple of bags of groceries could change lives, which is Center City Churches' overarching goal. I now conclude that the people with whom I share resources and blessings are grateful not only for food but also for the few minutes we have to relate person to person. My heart smiles when their faces smile, and we are both changed.

Regner Arvidson
West Hartford, Connecticut

**I think some of the biggest world problems** we need to solve involve racial, religious, and economic divisions. We strive to find ways to connect in a real way at City Year. We deliberately put together people who come from different walks of life. We believe that is central in the world that we must eventually create, where differences are still valued and interesting, but finding common goals is even more important.

AnnMaura Connolly
Washington, D.C.

**You don't have to be good at something to enjoy it,** and you definitely don't have to be good at something to make an impact. Frankly, my extreme lack of skills in certain areas has made more of an impact on the kids I work with than the things I pride myself in doing well.

For example, I can't play basketball to save my life. Once I was mentoring a kid named Anna who had many emotional problems and wasn't in the best physical shape. She was insecure, and I had a really hard time getting her to open up to me and trust me. I am an adventure counselor, so all my activities involve something like hiking, rock climbing, kayaking, or the sort. I tried everything I had been trained to do to get her to open up, but she hated the activities.

One day Anna's supervisor asked me to play in a basketball tournament, assuming I could play ball as well as I could bike or hike. Wrong: I was terrible. I slid all over the floor, and more than once I ran into a pole, a folding chair, or a basketball. I figured Anna would be embarrassed by me, but something about my public humiliation helped her connect with the other kids, and more than that, it put her in the limelight.

After the game we were pretty popular—I think all the kids expected me to play like a pro, and the fact that I was a novice was refreshing. This incident opened doors for me and Anna, and we worked together for a couple more years before I moved away. I still check in with her from time to time.

Bonny Beiter
Austin, Texas

# BE THE CHANGE!

**I got involved in volunteering** and mentoring in my sophomore year at Clark Atlanta University. I was a mentor to a girl in the sixth grade, and it was a great experience. We always stayed connected even after I stopped mentoring her.

SistaSpace Collective Inc. is a one-on-one and group mentoring program for girls in grades 6 through 12 that focuses on self-empowerment and encourages academic achievement, leadership development, civic engagement, cultural awareness, and personal affirmation. To learn more or to volunteer, log on to www.sista space.org.

After grad school, I was talking to some of my colleagues. We said, "Wouldn't it be great if we could mentor some young girls, occupy their time in a productive way on the weekends, and be with our friends, too?" We had our first gathering of SistaSpace on February 27, 2000. There were 12 women and 12 teenage girls, and we each decided to match up with one girl as her mentor.

I had no intention of starting a nonprofit. It was just a productive way to spend weekends. Six years later, it's grown into a girl empowerment program, covering everything from academics to sex education to career development. We focus on adolescent girls of color who live in Atlanta.

The program is year-round, on weekends. We have strong personal relationships with the girls. With SistaSpace, I want to make sure that a legacy is left in the community. The legacy is left with each one of the girls we work with. Each girl realizes how older women made a commitment to her, and that she needs to go out into the world and make the same commitment to another person. She needs to keep that commitment alive. For our communities to change, we all have to create an active role in change.

Candace Meadows
Atlanta, Georgia

**It was a gorgeous Florida day,** and we were given the task of taking the more mobile and lucid senior citizens out into the yard for exercise. We played music to engage them socially, threw balloons and balls up in the air, played with hula hoops, and did in-chair exercises.

Toward the end of one of the in-chair exercises I was helping lead, I leapt up out of my chair and started dancing a little to the music, not thinking much of what I was doing. In the midst of dancing, I heard someone clapping and laughing. When I turned around it was Rosa, a beautiful, frail woman in a wheelchair, who laughed like a little girl. I couldn't help smiling when she told me seeing me dance made her day.

Joanna Vasquez
Miami, Florida

**I served as a tutor at an inner-city** elementary school for four years. Each year, I'd request the worst disciplined student, and I got my wish with one fourth-grade boy. He was a regular at the principal's office—so frequent, in fact, that the school wanted to remove him from the program.

The next school year, the students would be moving into a new building, which gave me a chance to use this as a start for improving his behavior. We sat down and agreed that in the new school building, he'd have a new attitude and never get in trouble. At the end of the next school year, I went to visit the principal's new office and took him with me. He said that was the first time all year he had been in, seen, or visited the office. I was forever proud of him.

Mark Anthony Thomas
Atlanta, Georgia

## Voices of Change:
## Bob Nardelli

IN SPITE OF DAMP AND COOL WEATHER on a Saturday morning last fall, a work crew was geared up for a major job: blueprints—finalized; site preparation—done; equipment, tools, and materials—shipped; safety measures—in place; and team—all set. Hands were ready to build, and hearts were poised to do much more.

It was the final volunteer project of our Corporate Month of Service. Let's just say I began that month admiring our volunteers; I ended it in awe of them.

The Month of Service concept began in 2004 as a Week of Service. The idea was that by concentrating the efforts of volunteers from our company, our business suppliers, and nonprofits, we could multiply the impact we made in building better communities. The week was a resounding success. But for us, it wasn't enough.

If a Week of Service generated so much participation and impact, why not a month? Why not enlist a team of other corporations and nonprofits who had the reach, the resources, and therefore the responsibility to transform people's lives?

Throughout my life, every success I have been privileged to experience was really the result of teamwork. Of course, individual effort is critical to any type of win, but it's the team effort—in which the talent of one is multiplied by many—that is fundamental to extraordinary success.

After one volunteer day at the East Lake Community Park in Atlanta, a seven-year-old wrote, "Thank you for building this park for *me*." More than 700 volunteers had converged on the youngster's historic neighborhood to construct rock-climbing walls, slides, and swings; revive nature trails; refurbish a recreation center; and revitalize a nearby housing community and school. The project was the largest ever of its kind, but leave it to a child to drill down the enormity of the effort to a simple, individually focused statement of appreciation.

The sentiment was echoed again and again. I saw it in the faces of the youth at P.S. 46 in New York City, which was transformed by 650 volunteers who created jazz-themed murals and painted classrooms to give the elementary school a new look. At the Osceola County children's shelter in Orlando, Florida, 250 volunteers came out to beautify the grounds. Flood damage to Pittsburgh's scenic, 37-mile Heritage Trail greenbelt was repaired by 150 volunteers. Volunteers united in Sacramento, California, to build a KaBOOM! playground, giving hundreds of kids a safe place to play.

Even where Mother Nature mounted an attack, human nature rose to become itself a force to reckon with. While 250 volunteers in the Houston area were working at Shearn Elementary School, another 100 of their teammates were in Louisiana and Mississippi volunteering on recovery efforts for Hurricane Katrina.

It's difficult to quantify care and compassion, but the numbers—and the stories behind them—are revealing. In all, more than 75,000 volunteers participated in 2,000 projects during the Month of Service. These men and women were not appointed or nominated or elected to their posts as leaders of change; instead, they were *called* to serve. In their answer, they contributed more than 850,000 volunteer hours that touched 2 million lives.

We're looking for more volunteer builders for the Corporate Service Council. Want to join?

*Robert (Bob) L. Nardelli serves as chairman, president, and CEO of The Home Depot, the world's largest home-improvement retailer. Following The Home Depot's 25-year tradition of investing in local communities through volunteerism and charitable donations, Nardelli led the charge in the company's first ever Week of Service in 2004.*

# Voices of Change:
# Susan Loyas

Today's teens are filled with compassion and excitement to make a difference in this world. I have worked with hundreds of teens on many types of projects through the service organization Pass It Along, but one stands out in particular. It happened two years ago.

Youth Service America Day was coming up, and the group wanted to plan something big and different. Se we contacted a mission house in Newark, New Jersey, where we had previously mentored children. The pastors there told us they would love to have a mural on the building to help brighten up the neighborhood.

Our teens were so excited that our monthly meetings became weekly meetings. The mission house gave us the concept for the mural, and five teens sketched it out to fit on the 50-by-20-foot wall. Next they went out and found someone to donate the paint for the mural. They gathered early on a Sunday morning outside of a local grocery store to collect donations to buy food so they could have a block party for those living in the mission's neighborhood. We rented a bus, and each teen who came brought $10 to pay for their bus ride.

Our bus arrived on this Sunday morning, just as the mission was finishing the Sunday morning service. We all gathered in the back of the mission and began our visit with some great gospel music, and the pastor introduced us to the members of the mission. We were greeted so warmly and everyone was so excited to have us there. We received a tour of the mission, which included a visit to their soup kitchen, and the teens gave them the food they had collected. Then all the teens and members of the mission divided up into teams. The artists started the outline of the mural, while others helped set up tables and chairs for the block party and others helped prepare the food in the kitchen. People from the neighborhood started to gather outside the mission to see what was going on. Soon neighbors came over to help.

When the mural was outlined, everyone tried their hand at painting. The teens, members of the mission, and neighbors from four to 94 years old helped paint the mural. There was so much excitement in the air, and everyone was having a great time. Someone noticed there was additional wall space on the left, and the decision was made that anyone who wanted to add their handprints to the wall could. Mothers with their babies were placing their handprints on the wall, and one 94-year-old lady from the neighborhood placed her bright blue handprints on the wall. When she finished, she stood back admiring her handprints and told everyone that she will always be special and remembered on this wall.

The food was brought out from the kitchen and everyone sat down to eat. Some of the senior neighbors who rarely came out of their homes joined us for the meal, and a few homeless men who came over to see what was going on asked if they could join us. Of course, they were welcomed.

After we finished the meal, everyone helped clean up, and the teens played with the young kids. Just then the pastor announced that the children from the mission house had put together a puppet show for us to watch. We all went into the mission, and the kids put on a show for us, finishing it with the song, "We Are Family." Everyone got up, sang, and danced together.

*Susan Loyas has been with Pass It Along since its start in 2001. She is a full-time volunteer with the organization and has been a board member for over two years.*

Youth Service America (YSA) is a resource center that partners with thousands of organizations committed to increasing the quality and quantity of volunteer opportunities for young people, five to 25 years old, to serve locally, nationally, and globally. Founded in 1986, YSA's mission is to expand the impact of the youth service movement with communities, schools, corporations, and governments. To learn more, visit www.ysa.org.

# BE THE CHANGE!

**I would not be who I am** or where I am today had I not had the opportunity to serve as a child. It is absolutely critical to facilitate opportunities for youth to get out of their comfort zones and into communities. Young people have a propensity for openness and are able to get involved in such a passionate way, working for what they think is right. They "get" that the world is broken and that their generation has to do something to help make it right. Through their curiosity and engagement, they have the ability to really change the world.

Rev. Amanda Hendler-Voss
Atlanta, Georgia

**I think that the moral center** of any community rests, in many ways, with its youth. Until young people actually get involved in something—whatever the issue is—things move much more slowly. After they get involved, things start to take on an energy and quality of possibility that I think they otherwise don't have. There is a totally different vibe that young people bring to their work. This has been true throughout history, and it is true all over the world, as well as in our local communities. There is an entirely different dynamic that gets created after young people find their place at the table.

Claudia Horwitz
Durham, North Carolina

**Young people have the potential** to have such a tremendous impact once they become involved in service. Several years ago, I saw a need within my community: a need for an after-school program for kids, a need for mentoring opportunities for young adults, a need for families to be able to come together and build community. My desire to create change around these issues led me to found a YMCA while I was still in college. It was the first YMCA in Korean history that was initiated and led by young people. I have since started several other organizations in Cheonan, and I know that it would have been difficult to do so without the support of my family and community. Young people are full of the determination, compassion, and innovation needed to get things done. We need to nurture these attributes and support them in making an impact in the world.

Hye Ran Yoon
Cheonan, Chungcheong Man-do, South Korea

**Junior Achievement has taught me** how the power of a not-for-profit organization can change the lives of students by making them aware of their potential and how they can impact the communities in which they live. I've seen how teachers and volunteers have benefited by their participation in Junior Achievement. JA has also taught me that I'm fortunate to be involved with an organization that can bring the business community and educators together to help our children be the future leaders of our free enterprise system. As a JA volunteer, I can truly see the power of what we do each day.

Frank Steininger
Houston, Texas

**When I was serving at a local soup kitchen,** I wound up sitting down and talking to a diner about his life. He told me how he would go to the library and check out elementary math books and how he was working his way up to algebra. I thought that was amazing and wondered whether, if I were in his situation, I would have the humility to go back and learn elementary level math. He inspired me to learn everything I can and finish high school with strong academic scores.

Rebecca Frank
Westlake, Ohio

Ninety percent of homeless adults need a new, warm coat each winter because they have no place to keep one over the summer months. Each December, New York Cares collects more than 70,000 gently used winter coats and distributes them to thousands of men, women, and children who would otherwise go without. To learn more about this and other service opportunities, visit www.nycares.org.

**Every year in New York City,** we do a coat drive for the homeless and the needy. Last year we collected 87,000 coats and needed a warehouse to store them. One of my tasks was to get a phone installed at the warehouse for the coat drive. When I called the phone company to explain what we needed and why we needed it, the operator told me an amazing story. The previous year he was homeless and had received a coat from the drive. He said that he couldn't believe people would sacrifice such nice coats and that the gesture of selflessness gave him faith in the world again. So he began to get his life together, and a year later he had a place to live and a good job at the phone company. I thought to myself, "Just when you think it's only a coat."

Melissa Bieri
New York, New York

## Voices of Change:
## Connie Wilson Ambler

While teaching at an independent Atlanta secondary school, I once took a group of high school senior girls to a women's shelter in Atlanta. Our visit that day was part of our semester's inquiry into the causes and consequences of homelessness in Atlanta, and our work included spending time with women whose support systems had eroded to the point that they found themselves on the streets, many with their children. They resided now in a facility that helped them regain footing and reestablish a stable and interdependent life. As my students and I approached the shelter, we weren't quite sure what the day would bring. Our facilitator, who coordinated the center's community relations, had suggested that that my students might hear a few of the residents' stories and, perhaps, share some of their own stories in return.

Before we entered, one of my students expressed her anxiety. Would the differences between her current circumstances and these women's create awkwardness? Would her presence be appreciated or resented? Part of the beauty of service learning is that it exists outside the realm of the planned, controlled, and formulated. So what could I promise her?

Upon arrival, our facilitator explained that our visit would begin by our attending, as guests, a movement class offered regularly to residents of this facility. The class involved a series of physical exercises designed to evoke memories or thoughts and to invite participants to share their reflections in response. The eight of us joined about the same number of women there in the experience of moving—sometimes deliberately slowly, sometimes spontaneously in response to music within and without, sometimes while stringing rainbow yarn onto the floor into shapes formed by the intersections of each person's strand.

We giggled awkwardly at first in the face of our self-consciousness and graceless moving. But time and laughter eased us all into some comfort, and when the music stopped, we shared how one exercise or another felt, what memory or awareness it evoked. And here was the beauty that I have seen over and again when we educate young people through service: In each other's company, women and students both were more than the labels they wear—more than recovering or privileged, more than mother or child, more than friend or stranger. In the ways that our movements and stories echoed or countered each other's, we glimpsed that mystery within and around that transcends labels, broadens our sense of ourselves and others, and remembers something common that our separate lives incline us to forget. Despite our circumstantial differences, the happenstance of our particular lives, and the complex histories none of us chose, we share a common life. The parting that day was warm, and whatever anxiety we brought was replaced by joy, courage, and hope.

One year later, the very student who entered movement class with trepidation wrote an article for her college's alumni magazine about a service learning seminar she had taken her freshman year:

"My work at this agency taught me that our nation's homeless should not be defined by their current condition; they aren't homeless who happen to be people, but people who happen to be homeless … They are real people to whom we must show compassion based on our common humanity."

The freedom she had both enjoyed and enlarged that day by her presence in movement class called her to continue meeting, serving, and sharing a journey with others whom, apart from courage and initiative, she might never have known.

*Connie is a beloved teacher of English at Westminster Schools in Atlanta. She brings literature and poetry to life for her students and is committed to weaving people together across differences.*

## Voices of Change:
## Trevor Morrow

It was the e-mail from Continental Airlines confirming my flight from Newark, New Jersey, to Delhi, India, to Kathmandu, Nepal, that truly showed me just how far volunteerism can take you—not only in the distance away from your home, but in the changes and growth in your life. For me, volunteering didn't start when I booked the 17 hours of flights to the other side of the earth, it began a few years earlier, much closer to home.

With high school came stress, work, ups, downs, and constant change. I soon found that the one thing that remained the same throughout my four years was the need for community service. In my freshman year, I found Pass It Along, a nonprofit volunteer organization based in my hometown. I quickly learned more about Pass It Along and all it was doing in our area: everything from building, planting, mentoring, and helping the elderly and disabled to aiding other organizations in need. Over the next three years, Pass It Along became a solid part of my life.

As my senior year of high school flew by, I began to think about where my life was going. After accepting admission to my chosen university and flying to visit the school, I realized I wasn't the same person who had entered high school slightly unaware of the world around me. I wasn't the same person from junior year who was completely unaware of the choices I had. I wasn't even the same person from midsemester senior year who was unaware that following your passion is something you can actually do, not just talk about. My involvement as a volunteer gave me the chance to understand the power we have to make a difference in someone's life; I no longer ask, "What am I capable of?" but "What could I be capable of?"

I decided to defer my admission and spend my first semester doing volunteer work, this time outside of my community. I researched organizations on the Internet that provide global volunteer opportunities, then mapped out what would be the next few months of my life.

In late August 2006, I will be leaving for Nepal to work in an orphanage for one month. I will return home for one week, then go to Africa for seven weeks. I will spend two weeks in Kenya working with HIV/AIDS orphans, then spend the remainder of my time in Tanzania, working with an arts program, orphaned children, and small businesses.

I never imagined that my "first semester" would be spent traveling around the globe and helping others. Getting involved on a community level has made me understand that the need for help is apparent everywhere. Whether in a third-world country or in the town next door, service is needed. All over the country, organizations like Pass It Along are helping provide for that need. These organizations inspire you and make you see what you can be capable of.

*Trevor Morrow of Sparta, New Jersey, an 18-year-old graduate of the Sparta High School class of 2006, elected to postpone college this fall to do volunteer work in Nepal and Eastern Africa. He has never been one to allow his age to dictate his ability. When Southeast Asia was hit by a devastating tsunami in 2004, he organized a benefit dinner at Sparta High School that raised $2,500 for relief agencies helping children in that region. Trevor serves as president of the Pass It Along Youth Council and has been recognized by Representative Rodney Frelinghuysen as an outstanding student leader and volunteer.*

A NUMBER OF YEARS AGO, we asked a small cadre of volunteer leaders to develop projects that would meet meaningful community needs. Matt and Stuart were in their 20s and both worked in the corporate world. A nonprofit organization referred them to a family in which the mother, father, and son all used wheelchairs. Every time they left the house, they had to call a cab and depend upon the kindness of the driver to lift them down their stairs. Matt and Stuart pulled in friends who were architects and drew up the plans for a wheelchair ramp, then they purchased the supplies and materials. For the day of their project, Hands On assigned them 12 volunteers, none of whom knew one another. They worked all day, but, being novices, they finished only half of the project by the day's end. Frustrated and worried, Matt and Stuart let the volunteers know that this was the first time they had done this, and that they knew that folks had to go home. They said they would find some way of finishing the project later. To their surprise, every single volunteer agreed to come back the following day to finish the ramp. On that day, they completed a beautiful wheelchair ramp, and in a ribbon-cutting ceremony, they celebrated the first time that the family members were able to leave their own home independently.

Out of this experience, Matt and Stuart created an ongoing project called Ramps for Champs, and they set out to build dozens of wheelchair ramps for other families and individuals. Today, this model has been emulated across the country, and hundreds of wheelchair ramps have been built in the ensuing years. I have lost track of Matt and Stuart, but the inspiration of their first project is lived out in dozens of ribbon-cutting ceremonies each year celebrating the power of community to restore independence.

M.N.

IHAVE LONG-STANDING ROOTS in the town of my birth, Perry, Georgia. My grandparents were civic and political leaders in Perry and cultivated in us a strong sense of place and responsibility. I grew up in Washington, D.C., where my father (with the full support of my mother) served in the United States Senate.

I was surrounded by family role models of service, leadership, integrity, and commitment. As I grew up, I was given the opportunity to participate as a volunteer—spending a summer working with homeless children at Martha's Table (which helps low-income people in Washington, D.C.), participating in Habitat for Humanity projects in Appalachia, and serving as a mentor. At a personal level, I found meaning, fulfillment, and a sense of efficacy in my service work. I felt that I was gaining far more than I was able to contribute.

Upon graduating from the University of Virginia, I began to explore opportunities to serve, from the Peace Corps to the Carnegie Foundation to serving as an intern at PBS. During my search, I met a couple of people in Atlanta who were starting a new organization. The group of 12 individuals who eventually formed Hands On Atlanta contributed $50 each and their own sweat equity to create a new, dynamic, and flexible model for getting their peers—starting with young adults—involved in the community. They started by promptly outfitting themselves and their friends in Hands On T-shirts and organizing a few monthly projects ranging from house building to sorting food at the food bank.

When I met these 12 founders, they had been given a donation of $2,500 and a small space in a local business office, and they were ready to hire a staff person. I joined, with the glorified title of executive director, working 10 hours a week with a job commitment of a couple of months to get the organization going. What I discovered was a perfect match—a meaningful way of making a difference in my home state and the opportunity to grow an organization and a civic change movement, to work in solidarity with others in something that transcended ourselves, and to partner with a broad range of organizations, in an effort to strengthen our community. I kept having more clothes forwarded down to Atlanta and extending my stay.

Seventeen years later, I find myself with a full closet (and a husband—a Hands On volunteer—and two small children) and firmly planted roots in Atlanta. Over those years, I have watched this fledgling effort grow into a dynamic organization and volunteer movement that has truly shaped the civic life of Atlanta. Today, Hands On Atlanta engages more than 100,000 volunteers each year, ranging from young children to seniors; manages the largest AmeriCorps program in the Southeast, serving thousands of children daily; and has helped cultivate a new generation of leaders who are now leading nonprofits, running the city council, and managing major businesses.

I have also watched this civic movement ripple out across the country. Several years after we started Hands On Atlanta—which was based upon a similar concept that had originated in New York (New York Cares)—we found that there was a growing tide of interest in replicating this new approach to service. Our approach allowed people flexibility in scheduling, the reinforcement and social capital of working together in teams, an action and impact orientation through hands-on projects, a quality experience, and an opportunity for service leadership. This recipe was catching on, with burgeoning programs in Washington, D.C., New

York, and Atlanta and with increasing interest from other communities. I gathered with six other volunteer and staff leaders from these cities in a series of meetings in 1992 to determine what could be accomplished through our joining together. We pondered the creation of a national network that would allow for shared best practices and would help support leaders in communities that wanted to start similar efforts. We developed a broad conceptual framework for a national organization named CityCares (later renamed Hands On Network), and we were lucky enough to attract a significant investment from the Coca-Cola Company. This national effort was located in Washington, and a board was assembled that included representation from our affiliates and a small staff.

After helping create a national network, I turned my attentions back to Atlanta and focused on working with a terrific team of staff and volunteer leaders to build what is now perhaps the largest volunteer/civic action center in the country. I also was privileged to receive a Kellogg National Fellowship in 1995, which enabled me to spend three spectacular years in a network of change agents. During the term of the fellowship, I pursued a personal learning plan to explore the connection between faith traditions and service/social justice movements. I traveled around the world, staying and meeting with families struggling through the peace process in Northern Ireland and the Middle East; met with environmental and political leaders in post-apartheid South Africa; and visited with widows of the civil war in Guatemala. I was able to learn and reflect upon fundamental questions of meaning, exploring the central position of service in the lives of individuals and communities. These experiences helped deepen my commitment to the work of Hands On Network.

At the conclusion of the fellowship, the opportunity of shifting my focus back to the national possibilities of the Hands On movement emerged. After a good bit of organic growth—we now had more than a dozen affiliates across the country—it had become clear that our national organization needed to be restructured by its local affiliates. I took part in a strategic planning process that reimagined the national organization, moved it from Washington to Atlanta, and resulted in me taking leadership. The organization was mailed to Atlanta in a few boxes, and we were given the opportunity to build the national organization from scratch (with a $40,000 budget, two computers, and no staff). For four years I continued to manage both Hands On Atlanta and Hands On Network. For the last three years, I have dedicated myself exclusively to the national—and now international—movement. It has been a great joy to watch the growth of this exciting civic-change movement and to work together toward a shared vision of possibility with citizen leaders from around the world.

Over the years, I have found inspiration in stories of personal transformation. I have borne witness to thousands of individual chapters that together form a transformational narrative that is being written and rewritten in communities around the world. I have been buoyed by uplifting examples of individual change agents who have changed their worlds and changed themselves in the process.

I have also hit walls, made mistakes, and been greatly discouraged. The most difficult period of my work happened during the still-early years of Hands On Atlanta. We developed a project named Hands On Atlanta Day that involved the entire community in a symbolic demonstration of what people can accomplish when they join hands. But in 1994, a terrible accident took place on Hands On Atlanta Day. A city truck rolled backward at one of our park projects and killed a woman named Barbara Starr and seriously injured her husband, John. It was a devastating moment for all of us. We questioned our work and the future of the organization. I felt implicitly responsible. In the midst of the despair and anxiety, we kept our focus on supporting the Starr family, and we deployed volunteers in every fashion we could think of—from getting new eyeglasses for John Starr to helping transport their son, Matthew. I visited John Starr in the hospital with great dread. Upon introducing myself and expressing my condolences, he grabbed my arm and pulled me near so that I could hear him. With great anxiety, I leaned closer. He whispered, "Thank you for all that you have done for our family."

I was overcome. The power of communion and of the reciprocity of service was made real. The following year, John and Mathew Starr participated with us on Hands On Atlanta Day in a celebration of the life of Barbara. For more than 10 years, John Starr and I have talked before each Hands On Atlanta Day, and I believe that he has participated in every one since that tragic event. This coming year, the event will draw more than 17,000 volunteers in projects ranging from wheelchair ramp builds to playground blitzes. I always approach Hands On Atlanta Day with a bit of trepidation as well as a sense of wonder: We plan and implement national and international Hands On service events that involve tens of thousands of volunteers, but beyond the numbers and the logistics, the real stories reside in the relationships—the reciprocity, renewal, communion, and sense of accomplishment that is derived from working together to contribute to something larger than ourselves.

Michelle Nunn

Hands On Network is a growing family of organizations engaging more than a half million volunteers within and outside of the United States. To find out more about our network of Hands On Action Centers, or to volunteer, please visit our Web site: www.handsonnetwork.org.

## Mission

Hands On Network brings people together to strengthen communities through meaningful volunteer action.

## Vision

We envision a day when everyone is inspired and equipped to be the change they seek in their communities.

## Core Beliefs

1. Everyone has the power to make a difference in the world.
2. Effective volunteer action is a path to broader civic engagement.
3. Engaged citizens are the cornerstone of a vibrant democracy.
4. Service brings people together and bridges differences.
5. Now is the time for action, innovation, and impact.

# CALL TO ACTION

Hands On Network is at the forefront of a growing civic movement of people coming together to strengthen communities through meaningful volunteer action. Combining the urgency of the needs in our communities with an unwavering belief in the power of volunteer action to help individuals and to stir the nation, we are relying heavily on the "power of one," where individuals will be empowered to manage successful community projects. Hands On Network will support the mobilization of 6.4 million volunteers and 100,000 volunteer leaders by 2008. This campaign will engage volunteers in projects designed to have immediate, tangible impact on children and education, health and wellness, and the environment. We are in the middle of a people-raising campaign. Join us. Raise your hands.

---

Do you see things in your community, school, or place of worship that you would like to support, build upon, or change? Download a free Hands On Network Project Planning Guide for the organizational tools to transform your service activity into sustained civic action. Through service, Hands On Network encourages volunteers to learn more about critical issues and take increasingly greater responsibility as civic leaders. Through leading in service, you too can be the change you wish to see in your community!

Log on to our Web site: www.handsonnetwork.org/bethechange

---

**Boston Cares** 190 High Street, 4th Floor, Boston, MA 02110
Ph: 617-422-0910 Fax: 617-422-0911 www.bostoncares.org

**Chicago Cares** 300 West Adams, Suite 300, Chicago, IL 60606
Ph: 312-780-0800 Fax: 312-780-0801 www.chicagocares.org

**Greater DC Cares** 1725 I Street, NW, Suite 200, Washington, DC 20006
Ph: 202-777-4440 Fax: 202-777-4444 www.greaterdccares.org

**Greater Philadelphia Cares** 100 S. Broad Street, Suite 630
Philadelphia, PA 19110 Ph: 215-564-4544 Fax: 215-564-4543 www.gpcares.com

**Hands On Asheville** (Buncombe, a program of United Way of Asheville and Buncombe
County), 50 S. French Broad Ave., Asheville, NC 28801
Ph: 828-255-0696 x402 Fax: 828-255-8004 www.volunteerasheville.com

**Hands On Atlanta** 600 Means Street, Suite 100, Atlanta, GA 30318
Ph: 404-979-2800 Fax: 404-979-2801 www.handsonatlanta.org

**Hands On Bay Area** (South Bay Office) 514 Valley Way, Milpitas, CA 95035
Ph: 408-956-1448 Fax: 408-934-1472 www.handsonbayarea.org

**Hands On Birmingham** 601 19th Street North, Suite 205, Birmingham, AL 35203
Ph: 205-251-5849 Fax: 205-251-1160 www.handsonbirmingham.org

**Hands On Central Texas** 2000 E. MLK Jr. Blvd., Austin, TX 78702-1340
Ph: 512-472-6267 x210 www.unitedwaycapitalarea.org

**Hands On Charlotte** 1616 Central Avenue, Suite 200, Charlotte, NC 28205
Ph: 704-333-7471 Fax: 704-333-1866 www.handsoncharlotte.org

**Hands on Columbus** P.O. Box 1216, Columbus, GA 31902
Ph: 706-649-3384 Fax: 706-317-5377 www.handsoncolumbus.org

**Hands On Georgia** 600 Means Street, Atlanta, GA 30318
Ph: 404-979-2910 Fax: 404-979-2910 www.handsongeorgia.org

**Hands On Greater Buffalo** (program of West Seneca Youth Bureau)
2001 Union Rd., West Seneca, NY 14224
Ph: 716-558-3325 www.wsyb.org

**Hands On Greenville** 600 E Washington Street, Suite 610
Greenville, SC 29601 Ph: 864-242-4224 Fax: 864-242-0509
www.handsongreenville.org

**Hands On Inland Empire** (A program of Inland Empire United Way)
1235 Indiana Court, Suite 104, Redlands, CA 92374
Ph: 909-793-2837 x25 Fax: 909-335.2708 www.handsoninlandempire.org

**Hands On Jacksonville** (A Program of Volunteer Jacksonville)
6817 Southpoint Pkwy, Suite 1902, Jacksonville, FL 32216
Ph: 904-332-676 www.handsonjacksonville.org

**Hands On Kansas City** 8016 State Line Rd., Suite 206, Leawood, KS 66208
Ph: 913-381-2655 www.handsonkc.org

**Hands On Las Vegas** (program of Volunteer Center of Southern Nevada)
3075 E. Flamingo, Ste. 100A, Las Vegas, NV 89121
Ph: 702-892-2321 www.volunteercentersn.org

**Hands On Louisville** 732 West Main, Louisville, KY 40202
Ph: 502-561-5226 Fax: 502-561-5224 www.handsonlouisville.org

**Hands On Memphis** 174 Williford Ave, Memphis, TN 38112
Ph: 901-725-2132 Fax: 901-454-1898 www.handsonmemphis.org

**Hands On Miami** 3250 SW 3rd Avenue, Miami, FL 33129
Ph: 305-646-7200 Fax: 305-646-7205 www.handsonmiami.org

**Hands On Nashville** 209 10th Avenue South, Suite 318, Nashville, TN 37203
Ph: 615-298-1108 Fax: 615-298-2397 www.hon.org

**Hands On Orlando** 199 E. Welbourne Avenue, Winter Park, FL 32789
Ph: 407-740-8652 Fax: 407-740-4192 www.handsonorlando.org

**Hands On Palm Beach County** (A program of United Way of Palm Beach County)
2600 Quantum Blvd., Boynton Beach, FL 33426
Ph: 561-375-6621 Fax: 561-375-6666 www.unitedwaypbc.org

**Hands On Pensacola** PO Box 17184, Pensacola, FL 32522
Ph: 850-934-0489 www.handsonpensacola.org

**Hands On Portland** 2145 NW Overton, Portland, OR 97210
Ph: 503-413-7787 Fax: 503-413-7671 www.handsonportland.org

**Hands On Sacramento** 909 12th Street, Suite 200, Sacramento, CA 95814
Ph: 916-447-7063 x328 www.handsonsacto.org

**Hands On Thomas County** P.O. Box 252, Thomasville, GA 31799
Ph: 229-226-5200 www.handsonthomascounty.org

**Hands On Tampa Bay** 1000 N. Ashley Dr., Suite 800, Tampa, FL 33602
Ph: 813-274-0999 Fax: 813-228-9549 www.handsontampabay.org

**Hands On Twin Cities** 2021 East Hennepin Avenue, Ste. 420
Minneapolis, MN 55413 Ph: 612-379-4900 www.handsontwincities.org

**Jersey Cares** 10 Bleeker Street, 2nd floor, Newark, NJ 07102
Ph: 973-242-0033 Fax: 973-242-2133 www.jerseycares.org

**L.A. Works** 570 West Avenue 26, Suite 400, Los Angeles, CA 90065
Ph: 323-224-6510 Fax: 323-224-6518 www.la-volunteer.org

**Make A Difference** 5151 N. 19th Ave., Suite 200, Phoenix, AZ 85015
Ph: 602-973-2212 Fax: 602-973-9233 www.makeadifference.org

**Metro Volunteers of Denver** 444 Sherman Street, Suite 100, Denver, CO 80203
Ph: 303-282-1234 Fax: 303-202-1242 www.metrovolunteers.org

**New York Cares** 214 West 29th Street, 5th Floor, New York, NY 10001
Ph: 212-228-5000 Fax: 212-228-6414 www.nycares.org

**Pass It Along** P.O. Box 457, Sparta, NJ 07871
Ph: 973-726-9777 www.passitalong.org

**Pittsburgh Cares** 702 Oliver Building, 535 Smithfield Street, Pittsburgh, PA 15222
Ph: 412-471-2114 Fax: 412-456-2212 www.pittsburghcares.org

**Rochester Cares** 846 South Clinton Avenue, Rochester, NY 14620
Ph: 585-428-7231 Fax: 585-244-8142 www.rochestercares.org

**Seattle Works** 312 First Avenue North, Suite 200, Seattle, WA 98109
Ph: 206-324-0808 Fax: 206-324.0817 www.seattleworks.org

**St. Louis Cares** 910 N. 11th Street, St. Louis, MO 63101
Ph: 314-539-4284 www.stlcares.org

**Triangle Impact** P.O. Box 14608, Research Triangle Park, NC 27709-4608
Ph: 919-633-9623 www.triangleimpact.org

**Volunteer Baton Rouge** 460 North 11th Street, Baton Rouge, LA 70802
Ph: 225-343-8270 x222 www.volunteerbatonrouge.org

**Volunteer Broward** 1300 South Andrews Ave., Fort Lauderdale, FL 33316
Ph: 954-522-6765 Fax: 954-522-6770 www.volunteerbroward.org

**Volunteer Center of North Texas** 2800 Live Oak St., Dallas, TX 75204
Ph: 214-826-6767 www.volunteernorthtexas.org

**Volunteer Center of Southern Arizona** 924 North Alvernon Way
Tucson AZ 85718 Ph: 520-881-3300 x145 www.volunteersoaz.org

**Volunteer Central** 175 W. Ostend St., Suite 100, Baltimore, MD 21230
Ph: 410-366-6030 Fax: 410-366-6032 www.volunteercentral.org

**Volunteer Hampton Roads** 400 West Olney Road, Suite B, Norfolk, VA 23510
Ph: 757-624-2400 www.volunteerhr.org

**Volunteer Houston** 3033 Chimney Rock, Suite 460 Houston, TX 77056
Ph: 713-964-0229 www.volunteerhouston.org

**Volunteer Macon** 195 Holt Ave., Macon, GA 31201
Ph: 478-742-6677 www.volunteersolutions.org

**Volunteer San Diego** 4699 Murphy Canyon Road, San Diego, CA 92123
Ph: 858-636-4131 Fax: 858-492-2016 www.volunteersandiego.org

## International Affiliates

**Amsterdam Cares Bain & Co,** www.amsterdamcares.nl

**Hands On Manila,** www.handsonmla.org

**Hands On Shanghai,** www.handsonshanghai.org

**Hands On Zimbabwe,** Harare, Zimbabwe

**Melbourne Cares,** www.melbournecares.org.au

**Nelson Mandela Bay Cares,** Port Elizabeth, South Africa

**RioVoluntario,** Rio de Janeiro, Brazil, www.riovoluntario.org.br

**Volunteer21,** Seool, South Korea, www.volunteer21.org/english/index.asp

* As of July 2006. Please visit our Web site, www.handsonnetwork.org, for up-to-date information about out organization, affiliates, and national programs.

We at Hands On Network have learned some important lessons for volunteers to consider as they take their first steps.

**Take the first step:** Don't let apathy or inertia get in the way. Try something, and then try something else if it does not stick, but do get started. I recently met with a group of people who had made their way to the Gulf Coast in the aftermath of Hurricane Katrina. One couple told me that they had never had a more fulfilling experience. They looked back at the moment of inspiration—when the idea to go emerged—and said, "Thank goodness I did it. Thank goodness I came. Thank goodness I acted."

**Find and make a meaningful experience:** Find a place or a service that intersects with your greatest passions. Don't act out of obligation or penance. Do something that feeds you, and in return you will find that your power and energy to make a difference will grow.

**Join together:** By working for and with others, we will create solidarity that reinforces our own commitment, builds bonds of trust and friendship, and nurtures our spirit and compassion.

**Follow a pathway to greater participation:** Keep challenging yourself to find new levels of engagement. Be open to new opportunities and think about how you can extend your reach.

There are many things to consider as you begin, renew, or extend your commitment to service. But the thing that *is* guaranteed is that your investment will yield multifaceted and often unexpected returns.

Do you have real stories about volunteer service that would inspire others to get out and volunteer? Would you like to share your story with thousands of readers? If so, contribute your stories to the Hands On Network blog at www.handsonblog.org. The blog features stories of volunteers changing the world, tips on how to make service a family affair, and accounts of how volunteers have come together to share the responsibilities of building or rebuilding a community. Some will even be selected for publication in the next edition of *Be the Change!,* which will include more inspiring stories of volunteer service involving real people like you, your neighbors, your coworkers, and your friends. We would love to learn about our readers, and we think you would like to learn from each other. Share your story and inspire others with your success. Let us know how volunteering has made a difference in your life. Share your reflections with other volunteers who have been out in the field, or let us know of volunteers who have been there when you needed help. Here are some tips for sharing your story:

Think about your start in service. Who or what inspired you to get involved?

What defining moments come to mind when recalling your volunteer experience?

Who is your role model for changing the world?

What is the ultimate vision you are working toward in your civic engagement efforts?

How has your service created change in your life or impacted the lives of others?

What have you learned or been able to teach others through your service?

What tips or helpful ideas do you have for others looking to get started in service?

# ACKNOWLEDGMENTS

In the spirit that "hundreds of heads are better than one," this book has literally been created by hundreds of people. *Be the Change!* reflects the great efforts of Jayne Hallock, our lead headhunter, who interviewed hundreds of everyday heroes. Jayne was supported by volunteer headhunters, including Tori Bledsoe, Shelley Mann, Amber Smith, the Uggets, Marianne Farmer, Anne Vidal, Christine Junge, Linda Holtzapfel, Heather Leatherbury, Dawn Hampton, and David Jay Bolanos.

Fabiola Charles, Michele Reiner, and Melissa Devereaux played critical roles in collecting the thousands of stories represented in the book and pulling them together to create a meaningful and substantive narrative of change.

Thanks to our "kitchen cabinet" of advisers, including Jennifer Hartz, Beth Gluck, Debra Feldstein, and Julie Trell, who offered important feedback and advice.

Particular thanks also goes to David Hume Kennerly, who provided us with his moving photographs, and Tom Brokaw, who offered such a compelling foreword.

Mark Bernstein, as publisher and personal champion of the book, has poured his considerable energy, stubborn force of will, and creative vision into every page. It would not have happened without his commitment.

Finally, special thanks to the extraordinary people who were willing to share their personal stories of change. Their stories and counsel are touchstones for all of us in our search for meaning, purpose, and fulfillment.

Michelle Nunn

HOW TO SURVIVE GETTING INTO COLLEGE: By Hundreds of Students Who Did
(ISBN 1-933512-05-9)

HOW TO SURVIVE YOUR FRESHMAN YEAR: by Hundreds of Sophomores, Juniors,
and Seniors Who Did (ISBN 1-933512-04-0)

HOW TO SURVIVE THE REAL WORLD: Life After College Graduation
(ISBN 1-933512-03-2)

HOW TO SURVIVE DATING: by Hundreds of Happy Singles Who Did
(ISBN 0-9746292-1-9)

WHERE TO SEAT AUNT EDNA? And 500 Other Great Wedding Tips
(ISBN 1-933512-02-4)

HOW TO SURVIVE YOUR MARRIAGE: by Hundreds of Happy Couples Who Did
(ISBN 0-9746292-4-3)

HOW TO SURVIVE YOUR IN-LAWS: Advice from Hundreds of Married Couples
Who Did (January 2007; ISBN 1-933512-01-6)

HOW TO SURVIVE YOUR BABY'S FIRST YEAR: by Hundreds of Happy Parents
Who Did (ISBN 0-9746292-2-7)

HOW TO SURVIVE A MOVE: by Hundreds of Happy Dwellers Who Did
(ISBN 0-9746292-5-1)

HOW TO SURVIVE YOUR TEENAGER: by Hundreds of Still-Sane Parents Who Did
(ISBN 0-9746292-3-5)

HOW TO LOSE 9,000 LBS. (OR LESS): Advice from 516 Dieters Who Did
(ISBN 0-9746292-8-6)

YOU CAN KEEP THE DAMN CHINA!: And 824 Other Great Tips on Dealing with
Divorce  (ISBN 0-9746292-6-X )

HOW TO LOVE YOUR RETIREMENT: Advice from Hundreds of Retirees
(ISBN 0-9746292-7-8)

Become one of the hundreds of smart and funny voices of experience whose collected wisdom makes our books so great. Survived a life experience and learned a lesson from it? Keep a mental list of do's and don'ts? Know an amazing story that happened to a friend or relative? Tell us about it. Share your advice, get published, and join the hundreds of contributors to the series.

Click on **www.hundredsofheads.com** to:

 tell us your story, advice, or tip

 suggest a topic for the series

 read and comment on what others have said

 browse or order current books and topics

 find out how to become an official Headhunter (interviewer)

**www.hundredsofheads.com**

"The next 'Dummies' or 'Chicken Soup'… offers funny but blunt advice from thousands across America who've walked some of life's rougher roads."
—Democrat and Chronicle (Rochester, New York)

"Colorful bits of advice … So simple, so entertaining, so should have been my million-dollar idea."
—The Courier-Journal (Louisville, Kentucky)

"The books have struck a nerve. 'Freshman Year' was the number-one-selling college life guide of 2004 …"
—CNN.com

# EDITOR
# AND CONTRIBUTORS

**MICHELLE NUNN** is the cofounder and CEO of Hands On Network. She was the founding director of Hands On Atlanta, which has grown from a grassroots start-up in 1989 to become one of the nation's largest community-based volunteer organizations. Nunn graduated Phi Beta Kappa from the University of Virginia and has studied at Oxford University and in India. She was a Kellogg National Fellow and has a master's degree in public administration from the Kennedy School of Government at Harvard University. She has also received an honorary doctorate of humane letters from Oglethorpe University. She currently serves on the President's Council on Service and Civic Participation.

**TOM BROKAW** is the former anchor and managing editor of the program *NBC Nightly News.* Brokaw has received numerous honors, including the Edward R. Murrow Award for Lifetime Achievement, the Emmy Award for Lifetime Achievement, the Records of Achievement Award from the Foundation for the National Archives, and the Association of the U.S. Army honored him with their highest award, the George Catlett Marshall Medal, the first time it was ever given to a journalist.

**DAVID HUME KENNERLY** won the Pulitzer Prize for Feature Photography in 1972 for his photography of the Vietnam War. He also served as President Ford's White House photographer. As a photographer for news magazines such as *Time, Newsweek,* and *LIFE,* he captured historic figures and events such as Fidel Castro, Anwar Sadat, and the mass suicide in Jonestown.